# RELATIONSHIPS

With strings attached

By

Brenda Nomusa Molefe

*Memoir*

www.relationshipswithstringsatttached.co.za

info@relationshipswithstringsattached/

brendmo05@gmail.com

WhatsApp: 076 510 0800

Copyright © 2025 Brenda Nomusa Molefe

All rights reserved.

ISBN:

Paperback: 978-0-7961-2491-3

eBook: 978-0-7961-2492-0

# DEDICATION

I would like to dedicate this book firstly to my biggest fan, my friend, my confidant, my shoulder to cry on, my inspiration, my shero, and my reason for pushing harder and harder every day. You may be gone Ma but you blessed me with so much love and wisdom. Mrs. Jostina Alice Molefe my angel on earth and now in heaven, I love you. Not forgetting my dad too, Ntate Molefe, he would be my biggest PR manager right now, telling everyone about me and the book. I miss you both.

I would also like to thank my beautiful kids for allowing me to grow with them as I navigate life not knowing what parenting is but they make this parenting journey so much easier, fun, and beautiful. Angela, Tironontshi, and Zyon mommy loves you long time #TheBrendMos.

To my siblings, you will never understand what a privilege it is to be a last born especially with four warriors always looking out for you and for that, I am forever grateful to you always. Phumzile, Dodo, Mbali and Khanyi much love.

To all my friends that have been in my life, you all know yourselves I really do appreciate you and wish nothing but the best for you and your families.

To you who bought the book knowing me or not knowing me, thank you so much, may all the love and blessings locate you wherever you are. Forgive the spelling and grammar mistakes life happened.

Lastly, all Glory and honour is to God almighty, I am who I am because you loved me even before anyone set their eyes on me. Thank you for patiently waiting for me in the mighty name of Jesus Christ Amen and Amen.

# CONTENTS

| | |
|---|---|
| DEDICATION | I |
| INTRODUCTION | 1 |
| CHAPTER 1  I AM LOVE | 2 |
| CHAPTER 2  THE FIRST BETRAYAL | 6 |
| CHAPTER 3  THE CONDITION | 17 |
| CHAPTER 4  THE BETRAYAL THAT CAUGHT ME BY A FUNNY SURPRISE | 24 |
| CHAPTER 5  THE START OF SELF-DOUBT | 33 |
| PARTNER BETRAYAL TRAUMA | 52 |
| CHAPTER 6  RED FLAGS | 54 |
| CHAPTER 7  THE FRAUD I MEAN THE FAKE LOVE CONTINUED | 62 |
| REFLECTION | 84 |
| CHAPTER 8  I THOUGHT I WAS HEALED | 89 |
| CHAPTER 9  AN UNFAILING LOVE | 95 |
| CHAPTER 10 FINDING MY WAY OUT OF - THE DEPTHS OF DESPAIR | 99 |
| BONUS CHAPTER  THE FOREIGN LOVE | 102 |
| ABOUT THE AUTHOR | 118 |

Relationships with strings attached

# INTRODUCTION

Picture this: 5-year-old me, sitting outside on my favorite spot on my mom's front stoep (porch), surrounded by the warmth and love only a childhood home can provide. I was naively and eagerly excited about trying out something that I saw from a movie we watched the previous night.

With a handful of wildflowers, I had gathered from the garden, I played out my own tender dream. I didn't know the name of the flowers, but they were definitely not roses as in the movie, haha! I plucked each petal, one by one, whispering, "He loves me, He loves me not". As the kid I was, my young heart swelled with joy whenever the answer was "He loves me".

I yearned for that love and wanted more "love me's" so I kept trying whenever I saw the next petal would get me the "he loves me not," I wouldn't continue or would pull out both petals so that I could get the answer I wanted, "He loves me!".

There was no particular boy in mind or a deep understanding of what I was doing, but I was determined that as I grow older, I will definitely pick the right " flower" (man) who would truly LOVE ME. Little did I know, I was in for a crazy surprise of - Relationships with Strings Attached.

# CHAPTER 1

# I AM LOVE

The day I realised that life was not fair for everyone.

Let me introduce myself: My name is Brenda Nomusa Molefe, a mix of Sotho and Zulu cultures also known as, Zutho (although that is not an official ethnic group, I think it should be!). My father was Sotho, and my mother was Zulu, but because we grew up in KwaZulu Natal we predominately spoke isiZulu.

I was born and raised in a small town called Ladysmith, to a big family that was filled with lots of love and care. My parents had a beautiful family home in a township called eZakheni kwa C (Section). Our home was a cozy haven, filled with the aroma of my mother's delicious cooking and the sound of laughter and music. We had our ups and downs, but never have I felt unloved. This led me to believe the world was full of love and kindness, that if you give love, you will get love in return. But that was about to change in the most drastic but gradual manner.

I recall a university volunteer group training session, where we had to introduce ourselves and share whether our childhood was filled with love or not. I was eager to share my story, to tell everyone about my childhood and how loved I was. So, the moment came, and I was called to finally speak. There I was, standing and staring into their faces with a big smile on my face.

# Relationships with strings attached

I proudly shared my story of being raised by two public servant parents who, despite having limited means, showered us with boundless love. I beamed with joy as I recalled the short drives with my father in his minibus he used for extra income. Our laughter and conversation filling the air. How he would treat me to my favourite take-away, fried russian and chips smothered in vinegar and the memory was so vivid, I could almost smell the vinegar! With a deep breath and a broad smile, I remembered simple moments like sitting outside as he cut my nails, his jokes making me giggle. My mother, on the other hand, was a soft-spoken angel, who was ready to serve the community, day or night, even beyond her time of duty. Her kindness was boundless and our walks in town would often double in length as she greeted people, or they stopped to thank her for her selflessness. Some would even give her money as a token of gratitude, which she'd humbly accept, often forgetting what she had done to deserve it. I didn't mind, knowing I would get extra treats from the money she received.

I smiled as I recalled how my mother would introduce me to her visitors. She would call me and my siblings to introduce us to the visitors, something she did religiously with my father. The best part was how she would introduce me, her lastborn pride and joy. She would jokingly say that she would charge double for my Lobola (bride price) just because of how special I was to her. She would even say, "My other daughters can get married without lobola, but for Twana kaMa, I want double!".

As I ended my story with a statement, that I am "love" because I was loved by my parents and siblings. Oh, now I remember we had to give ourselves a name based on our childhood. At the end of my story, I was all smiles but then I noticed a girl was crying her eyes out. I was taken aback, wondering why she was crying. It wasn't a happy cry either; it was a heart-wrenching one. This girl was Zama. She was the life of the group, always making everyone happy. I always enjoyed her company but why was she crying because of my story? Almost everyone spoke but she never cried or reacted, what happened now? Two more people spoke after me, she was still crying but not as bad now. Her turn to talk came. What came out of her mouth changed my life.

Zama stood up, a silly grin spreading across her face. I was confused, wasn't she crying moments ago? She took a deep breath and began to speak, her voice steady. "Unlike most of you, I did not have such a rosy childhood. Mine was a childhood no child should go through. My mother had me at 15 and by the time she was 23, we were already four. I had to grow up very fast as at 6 years, I was looking after my two brothers and sister while she left us locked in a room she rented. It wasn't until I was older that I discovered the horrifying truth that my father was actually my uncle. He had raped my mother repeatedly, starting from when she was just 10 years old, until she became pregnant with me. She then decided to leave home as no one believed that she was raped by my uncle".

The room fell silent, as if the weight of Zama's words had sucked the air out of it. I felt a lump form in my throat, my heartache for the little girl she once was. The silence became so thick as she continued her story, "mom faced more hardships with three men who promised her the world but later left when she was pregnant. The last one, who stayed the longest, also decided to exploit her further, as he decided that I needed to be the woman of the house when he slept with me when I was just 12 years old. This abuse continued until I finished high school, and I obtained a scholarship to study far away from home. Although I enjoy my life here, I worry about my little sister. I'm not sure if she is strong enough to handle what's coming to her. I pray daily that this man spares her until I can rescue her once I start working. So, yes! That's a glimpse of my childhood. I think I would call myself a survivor cause my childhood was nothing but a battlefield that only the strong could survive."

We sat in stunned silence, our eyes wide in disbelief and our jaws dropped in shock. This was the saddest story I had ever heard. I couldn't believe that life could be so cruel. Yet, there stood Zama, strong and tear - free as she took us through her childhood. The tables had turned; we were the ones overcome with emotions, crying our eyes out. The session came to an end and the counsellor told us many comforting words. She reminded us that as we navigate counselling students, although it was career counselling, we will occasionally find ourselves doing life coaching and in that moment, we must draw strength from our childhood names. Later, as I sat in my room, thoughts of Zama flooded my mind, leaving me feeling defeated. I had wanted to reach out to her and give her all the love I can immediately after the class, but she reassured me she was stronger than the story and I should not worry about her.

While I had faced challenges and tragic experiences in my own life, it was nothing compared to hers. But was it really necessary for me to compare? Had my comfortable, love-filled life truly prepared me for the harsh realities of life? I started feeling vulnerable and thinking maybe I'm not better equipped for life suddenly as Zama looked like a conqueror. I've always been a happy soul and believed in the best in people. Here and there, I would have people misjudge me, because they did not know me but those that did, knew that I would move mountains for them so much that they would abuse my kindness. Life went on, we had the best career counselling year and never really had serious issues. In fact, I even forgot about that training session. But little did I know that the lessons from that day were to come out in my near future. Let's journey along together as I unpack my heart experiences chapter by chapter.

# CHAPTER 2

# THE FIRST BETRAYAL

*There were many but this cut deep because it came from a friend and practically sister because we had been staying together for almost or just over 3 years.*

*Before I get to the betrayal let me first take you through how we met and all we had been through together.*

It's January 2001 a very hot hot day, I was not used to this hot Pretoria weather, but I guess I was going to have to get used to it because this is where I will be staying for the next 3 to 5 years. My mom and cousin had just finished unpacking my last luggage from mom's car. They were about to leave me in this foreign city. Part of me wanted to cry but another part of me was looking forward to this new chapter of life.

My mother on the other hand was so nervous but had to be strong and trust me to make the right choices for my future. The residence (res) she left me in was not really ideal for her. We had applied for a female res closer to school only to find that they did not even look at my application, so my only option was to move into this mixed res far from campus and it did not look well maintained. The res was looking unkept because it was recently acquired by the Technikon (University of Technology in today's terms). There were ladies in another house close to mine, mom went there and asked them to look after me because they seemed older and looked like decent girls. Mom's judgement was never wrong because indeed those ladies were very friendly and made the transition to independent tertiary life such a breeze. Before they drove off mom told me, "Tomorrow morning go back to res admin and follow up on your application to stay at the lady's res inside campus", she was not really happy leaving me there. I waved goodbye and assured her that I will go there and to not worry I will be ok. After they left, I just went straight to sleep as I was tired from the long drive (Ladysmith to Pretoria) as well as cleaning my place up.

I was woken up by a knock, someone else was moving in. This girl was shouting and causing a scene as she was telling her dad that he can't leave her at res, her voice was so loud with a spoiled brat tone, she kept on saying "I cannot stay here please rather get me a flat in town or something I cannot stay here". The dad tried to change her mind by saying "but baby this is a decent place look at her she looks decent enough wearing her Political Party T-shirt, she is going to be a good roommate you will love it here". I just stood there confused. She refused and they left. I just heard her father telling her as they left that tomorrow he is bringing all her things he does not want any stories. I was like ok what was that and I went back to sleep. I had a long day, the timetable showed classes in rooms that were so far apart from each other I was going to need all the strength I could get. I slept alone that night, locked myself in the room because I was so scared. The next day I prepared to go to class. Just as I was about to leave one of the ladies that my mom spoke to came to fetch me to show me where to catch the bus to main campus. She was so sweet even took me to my first class. I told myself, "Ok this was going to be a breeze". The first class finished and as we were going to the next class getting lost in the building, I met 2 girls who were also in my class. We decided to get lost together, we laughed and got ourselves lost the whole day until it was time to go back to res.

The one lady was from Soweto, so she was commuting every day, and the other one was moving to the same res as mine. I was excited to know that I will be having a friend in the same res who also stayed at the same res. She had to wait for her sister to come get her, so I went straight to my bus. As I was sitting in the bus, I remembered I did not go to res admin "ohh well I will go tomorrow". I got to my place got comfortable and decided to make myself lunch it is at this time that I realised I had not eaten the whole day. "It was going to be tough if this is how life is going to be", I thought to myself.

Next thing I hear a knock at the door I'm thinking "it's yesterday's rich daddy's girl". I'm annoyed as I go open, why don't they just open they have their own keys just like me. Lou and behold it's the girl I was getting lost with, she was carrying two bags, and she could not open the door. We both screamed because we could not believe we were going to stay in the same house together. Her sister couldn't understand the excitement, but we could not contain it we were super happy. I helped them move all her things I was now the one showing her around since I had been there first. Even told her that I met our other roommate, and she should brace herself as she is a character and a half. The fourth roommate was planned to come in February as she was in her 3rd year. This was a great surprise, "life will not be so difficult after all", I thought. What a beautiful coincidence to be staying with someone whom I just met in class today. We chatted the whole time like we knew each other. The ladies from next door also came to greet her, everything was nice and rosy. The week went by we were going together to class came back and explored res. I kept forgetting to go to res admin I don't know if it was deliberate, or I just genuinely forgot. I would remember when my mom would call me and ask if I did go. Yes, I had a cell phone a very huge Erickson Alcatel hahahaha. My sister gave it to me since I was going far away. It ended up being our house phone because my other roommates did not have a phone, and we had to place it on one of the windows so that it can catch the network (hahahaha we are so grateful now for the cell phones with improved technology).

## Relationships with strings attached

Well, it was just the two of us for a while because the other lady ended up not coming. One day in between classes the friend from Soweto (let's call her Linda) started sharing her frustration with commuting to Pretoria every day and she was not winning with getting space at res. So, my roomy (let's call her Xola) had a bright idea that she must come stay in our spare room since daddy's girl has not come as yet. I supported her, I was like yah come through she doesn't want to stay there anyways. Next day our friend came with just few things remember she was not officially occupying the room in case the other girl comes, she had to travel light hahaha. Weeks went by and we stayed all three of us with no stress.

The next month our last roommate came (Lets call her Dee), she was so sweet and wise always gave us life and study advise. She was hardly at res because she always visited her boyfriend so the time, she would be around it would be great to be with her even though it was short because the boyfriend would also come visit her. Their love story was very inspirational and refreshing. Anyways 2nd week of February it was time for Xola's cousin to come to res as well, as she was doing a short program that started in February. The day she came we all went with Xola to visit her in her house which was in a different block from ours. When we got there her mom and sisters were still there helping her move in. She (let's call her Londy) was a nice girl my first impression of her was that she is beautiful and well taken care of by her family and they were tending to her every need, even did not see us as we came to assist her move in. Anyways now it was the 4 of us. Somehow Linda and Londy did not get along very well. For the first time our harmonious living was riddled with drama and fights. Most of the fights were centred around Xola it's like both of them were fighting to be the one closest to Xola. Well, guess our peaceful space was short-lived. At this time, I had given up on finding space at the ladies res. I was at home now here; I was happy and vibing with everyone.

We spent most of our time going to class, visiting friends around res. But most of the time we spent together, and we grew closer and closer. We did not have a fridge so we would buy meat and cook it same time for all of us to eat. Xola never really liked eating but she liked experimenting with cooking for us. One time I decided to buy lamb chops for all of us, after making it Londy was like she is not hungry I must not dish up for her, in fact, she was on a diet. I never really cared much about dieting and body image until I met these 2 (Xola and Londy). In fact, I guess at some point they messed with my hormones because I would eat and not get fat but since I started joining them in diets my weight just started fluctuating with the amount of food I eat ahahahaha.

Well back to chops. Linda, I and the other lady from next door enjoyed the chops while the lady from next door was telling us about ghost stories that are supposedly from the res we were staying in. We went to sleep happy saying we will have nice breakfast because there was still more meat left. When we woke up the next day there was no more meat in the pan. We knew Xola does not eat so we asked Londy if it was her, she said maybe it was Pieter the Ghost hahaha. It's still a mystery even today who ate that meat, but speculations were always around Londy. Another incident happened where I bought eggs and Londy on the other hand was complaining that her eggs were rotten. I went to class and when I came back my room was stinking, all of a sudden now my brand-new eggs were rotten and Londy was frying up a storm there by the kitchen. These are just instances that would happen, and I would let it slide but Linda would be livid and confront Londy and a fight would ensue.

One day we were walking to buy street snacks (that is what we called the cheap chips that they would normally buy in bulk and then pack them in plastics for re-selling) from another tuckshop outside res. We passed Londy sitting with her friends and one of her friends called Linda a witch. Me being me and not confrontational I tried to tell Linda not to do anything about it but she would not let it rest. She asked me to go with her to confront this friend, but the confrontation turned into a huge

## Relationships with strings attached

fist fight. Our peaceful place was completely gone now there was drama after drama until the year ended. At the end of the year Linda decided she will move out of her room and Londy moves in because clearly, they were oil and water, and she would always be around to visit Xola, and it was not going to work to continue this living arrangement. Luckily the swap was approved as Londy now qualified to move to our block and she had finished her short program to now start her diploma.

Well, everything was fine the drama subsided now it was just their fights as siblings/friends. I was happy to stay with them because it meant my hair was always on point and they were genuinely cool people to be around. They had more experience when it came to relationships then me that was a welcome learning experience. I had a high school sweetheart who would occasionally come visit me because he was studying at the University of Johannesburg. So, I never really had a chance to date anyone at res I would live vicariously through my roomy's experiences, and it was quite an interesting journey to watch. At some stage I was labelled uMzalwane (a zulu word for Christian believer) because I was not seen to be dating anyone, but I was fine just having fun and focusing on my studies. Maybe that's where I went wrong because out of the 3 of us, I am the one who did not get married, but I lived the "good girl" life almost throughout res time because I met the father of my kids on my last year at res but more on that in the following chapters. Well, the reason I penned this whole history was for me to get to my first big betrayal. So, as I said we were together for quite some time I think stayed together for 3 and a half years. On our 3$^{rd}$ year we decided to move to a different block where we then met a new roommate as Dee was done with her studies. We met with Samy she was a sweet soft-spoken girl. Londy was excited to stay with her because she felt because she met her before us at some party perhaps, she can have that bond with someone else the way Xola and I had a bond because we were doing the same course and stayed with each other longer.

## Relationships with strings attached

Time at this new block was ok not any major drama issues just the usual. On my side I was starting to feel maybe this high school sweetheart thing was not working out. I dated someone else briefly but that also ended after only 2 months. I stayed single and focused on my studies. High school sweetheart would still occasionally come but things were no longer the same. One day while coming back from res I met this very handsome guy he was new at res. I got to our house excited couldn't wait to tell my roommates they were all there. I told them about the guy. Londy was like who is this guy you're not the first one to say there is a new handsome guy at res. After that they made fun of me saying it was the first time that I mzalwane was so excited over a random guy. While I was sitting outside, I saw the guy, so I called them to come see him. They all ran outside, and they were shocked at how handsome he was. Guy was handsome handsome. Well, Londy took it to herself to do research on the guy. She would come with feedback that he is the younger brother of another lady we go to church with. She was good at "this approaching man" thing. Well, she was beautiful and confident, so she had everything working to her advantage. One day she organised that we go introduce ourselves to the guy, her actual words were that "I'm going to introduce you to him". You guys have similar personalities in fact he is so good that he is still a virgin can you imagine at his age so we would be perfect match with my mzalwane status.

Indeed, we met the guy and exchanged numbers. Guy started visiting our house quite often. Me being me I decided nope I want to take things slow we get to know each other etc. etc. So, we would chat almost every day, he would come to my room, and we would chat till late. Usually, I would never see him out as he would leave because sometimes, he would go to Londy's room stay few minutes then go. I did not see anything wrong with that she is the one that facilitated our meet up anyways. This went on for about a month or 2. Holidays came, and we all went home. While I was home our friendship or connection grew stronger or so I thought, as we would chat every single day.

## Relationships with strings attached

He would tell me that he can't wait for me to meet his mom she would really love me. So, this went on for some time till I came back.

When I came back, I decided to tell Xola as we were chatting that I think I have put this on hold for some time now, I will now accept Mr handsome's advances for us to officially be a couple not just friends. I showed her our messages throughout the holidays. Xola immediately got agitated she was like "you know what I can't keep this lie any longer". I was shocked I'm like what lie. She was like "remember when Londy asked you how would you feel if your best friend slept with a guy that you like and you dismissed her completely and told her it would be the worst betrayal because you value friendship so much. She wanted to confess to you that she was sleeping with Mr handsome". I have never been so shocked in my whole entire life. Here I was ready to take this relationship to the next level, I remember I even joked about moving from zero to 100 because I was not sure if I will make him keep his virginity after we have been flirting for so long. Xola said forget, that virginity was taken by Londy but please don't tell her that I told you. I will just keep pushing her to tell you because she says she does not know how to tell you because she can't find the right words. She also saw my messages with him and after seeing those messages she called off whatever they were having because she realised the guy was also now lying to her. I was really hurt and did not know if I could keep this inside me for long. I kept quiet but this was killing me, eventually I confronted her and the situation. I told her I can't really be friends with her anymore after keeping such information from me and doing such after she knew how I felt about the guy.

That betrayal really put a dent in my soul because it was so unexpected and brought out feelings in me that I never knew existed. I hated the ground she walked on. Suddenly all the little things she once did, and I overlooked became elevated. I went on "I can't speak to you for days". The situation was tense in the house like never before. Maybe if I faced the situation like

## Relationships with strings attached

Linda and physically dealt with it instead of emotionally dealing with it maybe it would have not cut so deep. It would have not taken me years to let it out of my spirit. But the young girl in me dealt with it in the most emotionally damaging way. I forgave her for peace in the house. I chose other people instead of me. I then later realized that mentally and emotionally I was not ok. Her and Xola moved out in the middle of the year. I guess it was out of site out of mind type of situation, but the betrayal was lingering in my subconscious. Now at this stage, I was questioning whether it was me or whether I was wrong for being upset because really me and the guy were just on talking stage more like friends. One day they came to visit, our old roommate Dee was also there and this time I had finished my studies looking for work. She asked Dee if it was better to get good marks and finish or just look for work while completing your studies because she could see that people finish and don't get jobs. The people in the room was me. I had been the only one among our friends that had graduated, and my marks were good however I was struggling to get a job. So, it was not enough that she broke my heart back then now she is mocking my situation of not finding a job, yet I was now qualified and doing my postgrad degree?

Clearly, nothing she says will ever sound good to me for as long as I have not fully dealt with the betrayal. I remember telling my niece's nanny all the hurt I was going through. She was so upset even said when you graduate again, I'm going with you I want to deal with this girl how can she hurt someone like you. I played the victim for so long till it drained my whole energy. Now it was hard to even trust any man that showed interest in me because I had this lingering betrayal in my head, if someone I was so close to could do such a thing how much more someone that does not know me.

One day for the first time after a long time I met a guy that I liked. We had met briefly 4 months before, but I think at that stage I was too blind to even see anyone. This time around this guy really broke down the wall and got to my heart. I remember

## Relationships with strings attached

telling Samy that I need to not delay this union before Londy gets to him too. That time Londy was not even staying in the same res anymore, but the damage was still lingering. At this stage I ask myself what if my judgement of this guy was clouded by his handsome looks and not wanting to be Londy's victim again that I moved too quick and dropped my standard of letting the spirit lead my decision. This relationship happened and lasted long but 2 kids later when things crumbled, I went back to the beginning and questioned whether I was soberminded when I made the decision to be with him.

Anyways years passed eventually I got a very good and well-paying job at the very first breakthrough of my job search. Guess what? Londy was the one to question that really was I telling the truth did I really get that Internal Auditing job without an internship or training. How can I be appointed for a job that needed 4 years' experience when I had none? Her comments went further to even make remarks about the type of car that I bought the first time I bought my car 8 months into my new employment. That was the last draw. That is when I decided I am going to speak my mind now. I wrote her a long letter explaining all my hurt I even remember I wrote that if she were my boyfriend I would have broken up with her a long time ago, unfortunately I thought keeping the friendship was good for everyone. I was no longer prepared to break my heart at the expense of keeping the peace among us as friends. I let that relationship go physically emotionally and mentally. I told her I forgave her just like how God expects us to forgive so she should not worry about that. I wished her luck and ended everything. And indeed, I never heard and encountered her anymore.

She would try to add me on Facebook, but I would reject her request. One time she wrote me a long text of how she misses me and that she is older now and realises her mistakes and would like to be friends again, she knows I now have a child she has a child too whom she gave the same name as my sister. I wished her well and maintained that she should be happy and be free, but we cannot be friends, with no hard feelings. I think at that stage it was still just words. I really felt freedom years later when we did an exercise at church to cut past hurt and her betrayal kept showing up over and over again and I cut ties finally for the first time in years. I had the perfect peace I had been longing for regarding this relationship. It taught me a lot about trusting God and forgiving from his word and from knowing that I myself was not perfect. I could now look at my past and present decisions regarding this situation with loving eyes. I now genuinely wanted her to have the same peace I was having and to also move on. We were young and still experimenting with life. For us to be friends again I was not sure because we were at different stages of life. She reached out again in 2020 but at the time she reached out I was going through a terrible time in my relationship I just could not even respond to her I just let things be.

What I learned from this experience is that forgiveness is more for you than the other person. The more you don't forgive the more it eats you up inside and makes you manifest even worse experiences in your life. When I was operating under that hurt, I made a whole lot of wrong decisions that got me stagnant in life and even cost me finding the love of my life, I guess. Betrayal is bad but it can hurt you more than the actual betrayal if you don't deal with it from the point of love and God's perfect peace for you and everyone involved.

# CHAPTER 3

# THE CONDITION

I realised when I started dating, I met a guy who was very handsome and very popular among my peers. We went to different schools, which made it easy for me as I was not going to see him every day as I was not sure of what I was doing. He was coloured (mixed race) so that was also a new experience for me. He would want to hug and kiss me in front of everyone (young and old) every time we would meet on Fridays at the Mall after school. If you would be aware of the Zulu culture, this was perceived as rude and disrespectful, so I would end up not wanting to meet him or refuse to participate in his lovey dovey gestures.

As I grew older, I realised that this is what my heart desired. That is my love language, but the societal CONDITIONS did not allow me to enjoy it at that time. I rejected it and unfortunately never got it back in any of my future relationships. That was my punishment, I guess.

When people found out we were together they were excited, they called us the perfect couple. I got scared and I let him go. I ended the relationship with no explanation or reason whatsoever. I had a crush on this guy for the longest time. I loved his smile, laugh and he gave the warmest hugs but because I was more concerned about "abantu bazothini" (what would people say) I let all that go. There were no cell phones at the time so we would only get to communicate when we see each other in town. So, I made sure I was less at the Mall and any other route where we would meet. I avoided him in every way possible. He would come to my house, which was a huge risk for him because I resided in the township, and he resided in the coloured area in town. I would watch him from my kitchen window and not go out. Even if he sends a child to call me, I would tell my younger cousin to tell the child that I was not around. At some stage, my cousin would trick me into coming out because he would feel sorry for the guy as he would stand for hours waiting for me to come out. I was a young foolish person, and I really didn't know what I was doing, but also, he got attached to me quickly.

There was a group of girls, who thought they were hot or the "it girls", who were shocked at how I landed such a hot guy. There was also a group of those that wanted us to be together. All of that made me want to hide even more. I guess I thought eventually he would forget about me. I mean I did not know what I was doing here. In hindsight again, I realise I might have missed out on a beautiful love story who knows. I might have found that flower after all and I threw it out before we got to the last petal of "He loves Me".

This whole situation killed him, he changed, started hanging out with the wrong people, and later got in trouble which landed him in jail while still in high school. I remember when news broke out that he was caught I did not believe it because it was so unlike him. My mom that evening started telling us a story of a young boy who was shot by police while he was trying to escape police custody. She went on to describe him as this handsome boy that was my age, in the same grade and it was so sad he got caught up with the wrong people. She went on to describe his family (it was a small town after all everyone knew each other) that's when I realised, she was talking about him. I was so hurt for him and shocked at the same time, also realised that I was too young for this, the way he was going on my

## Relationships with strings attached

parents were going to find out about us. Again, people or our peers made jokes that I was the cause of his wrong state of mind. I could not believe that I could affect someone like that if it was true. I was determined to right my wrongs in future relationships, no matter what.

The condition that cost me my beautiful princess love story.

Few years later, I met another guy this time he was not so handsome but popular in school (that was not my criteria I promise). He was just the first guy that I enjoyed talking to and I just said why not when he asked me out hahaha like no thinking or science was involved in my decision to date him. His CONDITION of our relationship was for me to know that he has another girlfriend stupid me I accepted this condition. He did not tell me right out front, I guess because I just said yes, the first time he asked me out I can't really blame him. How I found out he had a girl it was when one of my friends told me that there was a girl from another school looking for me high and low because she had found out that I was dating her man. She was waiting for me every Friday at the Mall.

*I feel I should explain this Friday at the Mall thing. I used to go to school with a school taxi. The kids had asked the transport driver to only pick us up after school on Monday to Thursday and on Fridays we would walk to town just to go to the malls, and we would use public transport to go home. We used to do this because the kids that were boarding also got a Friday to go to the mall so it was sort of like a social event and all high school kids from different schools would meet at either The Oval Mall or the other mini mall/shopping centre opposite the Oval. Ok, let's go back to my story.*

Now I've gone from running away from a boy two years ago to now being scared for my life because I was hearing horrible stories of how this girl beats the hell out of the girls that date her men. Every day it was like someone enjoyed telling me a new story of how this girl has beat someone up. There was one

Relationships with strings attached

incident where apparently, she waited for a girl that went to Ladysmith High school, by the mountain next to La Verna

Hospital. She beat her up and rolled her down that mountain.

If you are from Ladysmith, you would know how rough that route down the mountain from La Verna to Town is. Apparently, the girl was so bruised and needed some stitches. Was I not scared!!! Plus, I had never fought in my entire life before. One thing I was sure of is that I am not going to fight for no man, but I was so scared every time Friday came.

I then asked the guy about the girl, and he did not deny their relationship but just said he did not know how to tell me. I did not know how to handle this situation whether to dump him or not, so I just went along with our relationship which was us seeing each other every day as he was in our school in a grade above me. On Fridays, he would walk with me to town. But on this one particular Friday, my friend asked me to accompany her to pick up baby clothes and a baby bath for her sister who was giving birth soon.

I somehow had forgotten that there was a "sister girlfriend" still on the lookout for me. This was the day that she finally found me. We were walking with my friend carrying the baby bath laughing and thinking what if the girl pops up, did she not just pop up as we were laughing!!! My friend quickly took the baby bath and clothes. I guess she did not want them to be caught up in the altercation. She stood next to me as the girl started interrogating me. Surprisingly enough I was so calm, I guess in my head I had told myself welp it is what it is, just don't damage my face while you're at it because I ain't fighting back. She asked me if I knew the guy, and I said, "of course yes, the popular singer who does not know him'" (the guy had a name similar to a popular RNB Singer). She got angry and said don't act stupid I'm talking about the guy you walk with after school every Friday. I said "ohh him" he is just a guy from my school. She asked if we were dating, and I said "no" with a confused and straight face. She got upset, and said, "I hope you're not lying to me" and left. At that moment she wanted to say more but she held back, and I was so confused as to what was happening and she left. We also left to our taxi laughing and asking ourselves what just happened. My friend was making jokes that she was looking around as to what she was going to use to defend me. I on the other hand was not about to fight with nobody over a boy. The next Monday at lunchtime I talked to the guy about what happened on Friday, and he said, I know what happened I saw everything. Me and my friends came to you and your friend as someone told us that they saw us walking in the same direction where she was. So, they were watching us talk the whole time. I was like so you guys wanted to watch us fight that was not about to happen sorry. And he said that they watched yes but when he realised that the girl was getting upset, he came closer, that was when she left. It then explained how she left so abruptly.

So apparently, they broke up that day. Because the next Friday she saw us walking together and she said nothing to me or even greet him. Even today I cannot tell you what was happening in my mind during that period of the relationship. I don't know if I was 100% comprehending that I was ok to be dating a guy with another girlfriend. That I was nearly beaten up for a boy, but I was so cool and calm about it. Even after I was approached and told to stay away from him, I still carried on like there was nothing wrong. Maybe it was because there was no sexual attachment.

We dated for over two years without even thinking about sex and the time we did talk about it I was not ready to engage in such. It was not until his matric dance that I eventually agreed. We went on to be together until we broke up on my last year in my undergrad. In the time we were together there were few times that girls called me to tell me to leave their man alone. The last straw was when a girl called me after I had sent him a message at night. She told me I must leave her husband alone. Of course, he denied the girl, but I guess the wounds were now too deep. He begged me not to leave him as he had already told his parents that he wants to marry me even his grandfather has given him some money that he was to add on to start the lobola negotiations, but I guess I was already not in the relationship mentally anymore. There were too many strings attached to it that I could not be carrying them to my future. I had stayed too long in this relationship maybe because I was trying to not do what I did to the guy that ended up being in trouble with the law. But I had ignored my feelings and what I really want in a relationship for a long time. He went on to marry the girl that called me I guess, because 2 years after our breakup he was married.

Now I realise this shaped my future relationships. I accepted wrong conditions no matter how hurtful they were to me. When I eventually let that boyfriend go, after years of dating I met a guy who wanted to marry me from our first date. He was so excited to be with me that I knew all his immediate family members, friend's, mom etc. But the bad CONDITIONING in my head could not handle the relationship. I let him go just because he wanted to marry me. Stayed single for some time and met someone that I think I fell in-love with immediately, he came with the CONDITION that he would never marry me because we came from different cultural backgrounds. Wow crazy me stayed in this relationship for more than 10 years. Where someone was happy and constantly searching for a match and me on the other hand, I was a sometimes-happy bystander. One day he decided to propose because I guess maybe he was tired of looking. I had the most beautiful ring but that was just it a beautiful ring that I wore for 5 years until one day I decided to box it. When I did that, he went crazy and started accusing me of dating a foreign guy. That was in 2013 like the obsession he had with this idea was so scary. That time I had no foreign friends the only foreign connection I had was a guy who used to produce music for me years before I met him. I could not believe his accusations because here was a guy who could not even tag me on his Facebook status accusing me of cheating. I remember one day he logged into my Facebook account and posted a photo of us just for control, but that photo was on my "timeline" only, he did not even tag himself. I just laugh at this social media love concept and how my relationships evolved from no cell phones to fighting about Facebook posts. Anyway, that is when I realised the ring was just a block for me to not meet someone else while he continued his search.

One day on the Gautrain, I met the guy who once wanted to marry me and I was wearing the ring, he commented like "wow your married!!!", there was so much hurt in his eyes I could not believe he still had hope in us. That time I was hurting inside because the one I was with came with a condition. Fast-forward to current........... well, you are going to have to journey along with me to get the full story.

## CHAPTER 4

## THE BETRAYAL THAT CAUGHT ME BY A FUNNY SURPRISE

*I just need to take you back to that day for you to fully understand this chapter. It's funny now but it was not funny at all when I finally came to the realisation of the Betrayal. Here goes:*

Today was just one of those days where everything was just going right in my life. My skin was glowing, bank account smiling, and I had just been paid. I took the long walk to Sunnyside to do my hair. You know those African sisters knew how to bring out the African beauty in you. So nje my braids were popping. I decided to make them long and black so I was that yellow bone that you'd hate but just can't help but fall in love with. Wait, the day was just getting even better it was baes birthday tomorrow and you know what that means "birthday sex tonight". We going to be singing "It's your birthday and I know you want to riaaaade! birthday sex birthday sex" (singing my favourite birthday song in my head if you know it then you are too old like me hahahaha). Anyways I was a mood all by myself. I got to my place at res, and I called bae. I told him listen tonight it's me and you, I'm coming over I've been buried in books for too long and yes it paid off I passed all my tests. Tonight, I'm all yours I want to be buried in you. He got excited, or maybe, I don't remember but all I knew was that it's me and him tonight!

## Relationships with strings attached

I took a quick shower and put on my sexy lingerie, my tightest jeans, lace top, my cleavage was on fire, and I put on a tight Jean jacket because it was a bit chilly. I closed the whole look with my bright Nike takkies. Yoh, I looked in the mirror and was like dam girl uyababa (you are looking hot) today. I was that hot girl that even when I walked in the room the ladies would stand up and give up their seats for me and say Royal Highness queen have your seat hahahaha like everything was aligned and I was feeling myself.

I got to baes place and his friends were like wow bro where have you been hiding your girl dahmmm. I was enjoying the attention as inside I was saying don't stop boys keep the compliments coming. I was so hyped and even ready to go out which was something I hadn't done in a long time since I started working. It's been hard juggling work and evening classes. On weekends I was at a driving school, girl was focused and couldn't wait to buy her first car. But tonight, I was finning like getting drunk and my "cake" eaten like groceries! I've been a good girl I deserve it.

As we were planning our night, another guy came knocking, he answered the door and said it was Tshepo. I've heard about him a lot but never met him. He had been a good older brother type friend to bae since he moved to this new boy's res. Well, he came to invite the guys, they were having a house party by his place celebrating something I don't remember. Everyone was game we prepared to go there without thinking. I have money just got paid I asked if we should bring something, he said nah don't worry just bring yourselves.

When we got there, it was not packed. It was just a nice, chilled vibe with few guys and girls. Remember I was looking super-hot today. When we walked in all attention was on me and I was loving it hey and I got the hottest nigga on my side what more could a girl ask for.

## Relationships with strings attached

I was enjoying the environment we were having chilled conversations kumnandi nje (just vibes). I was all over boothang that day. I think my hormones were on overdrive maybe I was ovulating as I could not keep my hands off him. Someone complained about booze then Tshepo said don't worry Kat is coming with the booze. Bae looked surprised and asked "ohh is she also coming?". Tshepo said "yeah she offered to buy booze, too sweet of her right?" A few minutes later Kat walked in, immediately she took over the environment she was loud and smiling talking to everyone saying, "tonight you're getting high on my supply". Bae stood up quickly and went to help her with the box she was carrying full of booze, two other girls were with her carrying more plastics.

She saw me on her way to the kitchen she was like "wooou who is this gorgeous lady I've never seen her before?". Bae introduced me, she was like "wow girl where have you been hiding, we party with this guy every weekend I didn't even know he had a girl". I laughed it off "no been busy trying to juggle work and studies you know". She was like "yoh your just like my boyfriend you must have fun sometimes life is too short. Today I'm not complaining though because he bought us all this booze and we going to have a good time let me go make you a drink". She then told or rather ordered bae to help her. He jumped before she could even finish the sentence, they both went to the kitchen.

I was sitting there looking at them give each other glasses, girl was too comfortable with my man haibo (what!). They were laughing like it's just the two of them in their kitchen making food after the kids have just gone to sleep. It was like they've done this a thousand times he was giving her the different white spirits, she was mixing them, they picked up the ice together and laugh out loud as she puts it in the glasses, and she added pink tonic on mine and added coke on his. She gave me the glass and said I hope you enjoy it, it's our favourite drink. "Your favourite?" I ask, and she said "yeah, we make it almost every time in Tshepo's house before we go to Barceló's for a good time. We get there nice and tipsy. You should come party with us next time stop being too responsible". I took a sip and deep down wanted to hate it but damn it was too good just what I needed. After a few sips I was like this girl is a vibe maybe I'm just sensing the wrong things, she did say her boyfriend bought her these booze and she kept talking about him. There was no chemistry between her and bae I was just seeing things.

Party was a vibe I was having a good time and still all over bae like a sick puppy kumnandi man. Kat was still hanging around us, the smokers would all go out and smoke then come back every time. Bae also smoked and I hated the smell of cigarettes so I would stay behind and watch him, and Kat go out as they laughed and shared the cigarette while telling me ngyabora (I'm boring). They were too comfortable man even becoming the booze supply duo. Something was not right here ayi (no) man. She kept making comments like "dude really, you've been hiding such a beautiful lady. How long have you guys been together"? I felt the need to tell this girl we've been together for a long time. I didn't understand why bae had kept me a secret. "Well Kat we have been together 1 year going on 2 but that it was our first time staying in separate places. I had to move to this side because it was better for me for my evening classes and catching the taxi for work in the morning. I'm so lucky that he moved with me but could not get space where I stay but I'm not complaining he is still right next to me I see him every day". She was like ncoooo so sweet I still can't believe you've been letting him party alone all this time girl you're strong". I looked at the time it was almost 12, I tell bae I'm tired it's time to go. But deep down I was saying dude its almost 12 it's time for our birthday sex phela we do the most every birthday, 12 o'clock must hit with Mr. D inside. Bae was not having it he wanted his friends to sing him happy birthday. Kat had even lined up drinks for 12 o'clock cheers. I was now pissed we were going to break our tradition because of this girl that I just met today!

## Relationships with strings attached

Midnight hit and we sang and celebrated, she came and gave him a huge hug and kiss on the chic - hee did my eyes deceive me what did I just see now? It looked like she wanted to lend that kiss on the mouth. Tshepo saw the tension and suggested that the party move somewhere else and tells us, "See you tomorrow I know you love birds want to do other things. Tomorrow noon come back for brunch still plenty of booze and meat left". Kat says "haa guys why are you going to sleep so early anyway enjoy your birthday sex thina we not sleeping tonight".

We were home finally, I was happy wet, and I could not even wait to ride my man, the plans I had for him were even too wild for me.

Despite my little insecurities with Kat, I had a great time exactly what I needed. I told bae that with a huge smile on my face I had a good time as I tried to unbuckle his belt. He gave me a long kiss and then said, "baby I forgot something by Tshepo's place let me quickly get it, I'm coming back". I was too tipsy to argue. But was like babe could you not get it tomorrow remember they said they were going somewhere else? He said I know but he never leaves his house locked let me get it quick nawe (but you) why did you want to come home we could still be having a good time. He pushed me away and said I'll be back in no time. I just took off my clothes and got inside the blankets and told him to come back quickly been thirsty for him the whole day. He played my favourite music then he went out. I was in heaven; the blankets were so warm that I passed out the same time.

I woke up it was 5 am, and bae was still not back. Ehh what just happened? I called his phone it was ringing. I asked myself what was going on and I was in disbelief. Bae never ignores my calls where was he, so he left me sleeping in his room, really did this just happen to me on my slayest and horniest day! I called again now a woman answered I was like "hey who is this answering baes phone", she stutters and says "mmhhh sorry

## Relationships with strings attached

babe its Kat", and then the phone died. I call it back phone was now off.

While I was still there puzzled 5 or 10 minutes later bae walked in carrying Kat's phone, he just pretended he was too drunk and threw himself on the bed. I was fuming and didn't buy his drunk story. I tried to wake him up he didn't, so I decided to get dressed and go back to my place. Still not believing that "this guy just left me sleeping in his bed while he went missing the whole night on his birthday!!!". I took the phone he came with. I got home and I was furious. I called his number again now it was on. The girl started crying "Please where is your man he took my phone by mistake, and I took his. My boyfriend is going to call any minute, and he will be furious". I asked her "how did you guys switch phones because he uses a Nokia, and you use a Samsung there is no way you can make a mistake?" She dropped the call. When I called back, she no longer answered my calls, she sent a message, *please ask your man and tell him to bring my phone.*

Bae came a few minutes later now carrying his phone and angry that I took Kat's phone. He did not want to tell me what happened he just left rushing to give Kat her phone. I was left in my room angry and confused. What just happened here is this happening to me did I just witness bae rushing to get to another woman and leaving me here with so many questions?

I decided to take a quick shower to calm my nerves. After the shower, my roommate came to my room. She praised how cute I looked. At this stage I had even lost yesterday's Mojo I felt like an 80-year-old woman. I thanked her and asked her if she wanted food as I felt like cooking, she was like yeah man I can help you, is your man coming back I don't want to intrude phela you too are always all over each other. I laughed it off and said hayi (no) man let's go and have nice food. I bought some good meat and veggies from woollies let's have an expensive feast. I also bought wine and chocolate let's have some while we cook. My roommate always had a way of making me feel good I even forgot the drama that was happening in my life. I did not tell her anything because I was still confused. The food was coming along well even another roommate decided to join us. It was not always like this I've seen some struggle years throughout res life it was so nice that during my last year at varsity, I got a job, and I could spoil myself and my roommates. I hadn't known them for a long time, but they were good people. A bunch of crazy girls with different personalities. One girl was a lesbian she always had girls over, and she was the sweetest ever. One time she had a visitor and bae slept over that day. The house mother and res huckers (leaders) decided to do a spot check in our house that day and we were both in trouble. She was more worried about bae not getting hurt because he had to walk a long distance to his res which was far away before he moved to a res next door. We both lost points that day but she was busy comforting me, but I did not need them it was my last year in varsity.

Then there was another girl a nerd of note who was now a serious Christian that used to be a Rastafarian. After her mom passed away, she got comfort in the Rastafarian life but later on in life, she found God in this other church that did not cut hair and wore long dresses. But with all that she was fun to be around she also studied computer engineering with bae so they would sometimes exchange notes, and she always used to praise how bae was so clever he was the only black in a robotics class.

Then there was Palesa she was a supermodel who always entered beauty pageants and won great gifts. She was living her best life dating a guy who came from a rich family and driving a sports car. She was also cool to be around and shared so many crazy stories about her supermodel life. There was another roommate who was more of a Lokshin Barbie, she hardly came out of her room if she was around which was a few days a week. She was always at her boyfriend's place the guy looked like a ginsa (car hijacker in South African Slang) so we were all scared of him.

## Relationships with strings attached

Notice how I decided to tell you about my roommates that is how I escaped the drama of that day and completely forgot about all that was happening. I guess that is how God saved me from depression because I knew from a young age to compartmentalize all the things that happened in my life so that I don't miss any chance of happiness over something that had happened and was not actively happening at that moment. I still do that even in my old age, it has kept me from a lot of mental breakdown moments.

We finished eating I then decide to go watch TV in my room. I heard the door opening, it was bae. My heart sank because man I loved this guy, but I couldn't believe he did what he did to me. I immediately started shouting asking what happened. He just said I decided to go with the guys I did not want to sleep you're the one that was busy rushing to go back home. Ehehe did this guy just say that really? Did you leave me in your room to go party? Why did that girl answer your phone what's happening between you guys? He became defensive and said nothing happened and that the girl has a boyfriend their phones got mixed up somehow while they were partying. I didn't buy this story one bit, but I let it go since I did not have any proof and bae was not interested in telling me anything. I just said I don't want you to party with that girl anymore he agreed quickly and the next thing I knew we were having crazy sex.

The next day as I was going to class I saw this girl she was young but carrying herself like an old person, today she was wearing a different wig I almost thought it wasn't her, but she was with the 2 girls she came with that day that's how I knew for sure it was her. I greet them and she was acting weird not the bubbly girl I met the other night. Now I knew for sure something happened that day. This girl slept with my man something he denied for years until one day he admitted it when we were arguing about another girl he cheated with. This was just one of many cheating stories I tolerated in my 10-year relationship with my baby daddy. Maybe one day I will write a book "mjolo the sequel" because wow guy could not stop

## Relationships with strings attached

cheating. You would think this is what broke us up but no. I will tell you about it when I decide to write about it in my next book.

'

## CHAPTER 5

## THE START OF SELF-DOUBT

It had been 3 years since my long-term relationship ended. It took me a long time to find my feet and love myself again. This was a relationship that I was in so deep that I even forgot who I was. It got so bad towards the end, there were times when I was even fearing for my life as well as my kid's lives. It was not always this bad, he was a loving partner and father to our daughter hence it was not difficult to give him another child despite the challenges we were having at the time. Unfortunately, things changed for the worst, and I had to end the relationship when my son was almost 2 years old. This story is not about him maybe one day I will be able to write his story. I want to paint a picture of where I come from to where I am right now. It will all make sense when we both get to the final destination of my intention to write this chapter.

Ok let's go back to the beginning. 3 years had passed right, and I was starting to feel human again. I had come to terms with my decision to be a single mother of 2. It was time to start taking care of my health again. I looked for my taebo workouts because I was not about to go pay a gym membership that I never really commit to. I found my workouts and every morning before work I started doing my 30-minute sessions. I was feeling really good indeed the workouts worked fast also in just 2 weeks I was losing weight, and my skin was starting to glow different. One

## Relationships with strings attached

day in the office my boss introduced me to this weight loss program that was so easy but had great results. I joined and the weight started melting away so fast. Everything was starting to feel completely different I was happy and content. As the weight was melting off, I started changing my wardrobe and gave away few old clothes just to get rid of old energy as I accept the new. I was now looking and feeling good from the inside out. One of my colleagues was like "girl you really look good in every outfit you wear, you should try and join a modelling agency for plus size ladies, you would do great". I just laughed it off, but she kept on insisting even sending me plus size model competitions. I finally gave in a joined an agency in Durban with a branch in Johannesburg. I mean what do I have to lose but gain more confidence and now had something to keep me busy over the weekend since I had recently completed my PostGrad and Master's Degree at the same time.

The new model journey was fun but me being me I had to go and open my own modelling agency. This journey was also so easy fun and came with more confidence. You would thing I would be satisfied with whatever I was achieving. But I still had that longing for a companion, someone to share life with. Well, my friends and I were talking about how it's time I try and be open to new relationships. While I was not so sure the idea started weighing heavy in my mind.

One time when I parked my car at the Gautrain parking lot there was already a car waiting and this guy approached me saying "I told myself that today I will wait for you, and I will have a conversation with you". I just laughed and told him your welcome to join me I'm having a good morning anyway. I don't normally talk in the morning but today I'm in a good mood. We walked together to the train. We had such a great chat. He was working for one of the biggest insurance companies in Johannesburg, so we were both going to the same destination since I also worked in Johannesburg. When we got to Park station, he asked for my number, and I gave it to him without hesitation.

Relationships with strings attached

I forgot to tell you about him, he was tall, handsome, a little light skinned he had a small beard kind of resembled common the American rapper. I had been out of the dating game for more than 10 years now so did not know what to expect after giving him my number. Immediately when I got to the office, I got a text from him saying 'hey, I don't know how I will work today but I just can't stop thinking about your smile and that beautiful voice of yours, Volte (not his real name but close) from the train'.

Right there and there I was in heaven clearly; we were both not going to work today cause immediately my investigating skills started kicking in. I searched his number and name on the internet. Google never fails, his details came up immediately. There he was, LinkedIn said he was the head of the unit for this insurance company he told me about. I got excited a whole boss ok. Then there was a website of an engineering company that he was one of the founding directors. I was sold already. He also liked to study judging by all the qualifications he had. I failed to find relationship status because it was not on the net. I saw something that looked like a family vacation and that was 3 or 4 years back. Because I was sold did not want to dig further. I forgot that I did not respond to his message until another text came from him. He was now asking if he can WhatsApp me or call me and why am I not responding as he would really like to take me out for dinner Thursday night. I looked at the message and immediately started having an anxiety attack. I was like Thursday night is just day after tomorrow what was I going to wear and how was I even going to behave since it's been a while that I went on a date, with a complete stranger to top it off. I called my friend Sindi, she was so excited and shouted at me, "girl you better answer that call or reply to the message, one of us has to go out it's been a while I'll even baby sit'". At this stage I even forgot I had to find a babysitter and Sindi just thought ahead for me just like that. I finally responded and said, "sorry was busy in meetings but yes you can WhatsApp me". I immediately got a WhatsApp "please let's have dinner on

## Relationships with strings attached

Thursday?". I responded immediately "yes why not, I really enjoyed our conversation this morning". He replied immediately, "Great I can't wait, now I can work. Enjoy the rest of your day babe". I looked at his reply stressed out, "did he just say babe like seriously is it normal now to just call a random person babe?" I just replied with a "thanks you too".

My friends if my ancestors were with me, they were going to tell me run with both your feet touching your bums, but I guess had to walk this journey for some reason.

Later in the day I get a "hope you got home safe, enjoy your evening". I replied and that was the last I heard from him. I was fine with it cause at this stage I was starting to get overwhelmed and stressed about Thursday night and it was still Tuesday. Next day I also get a good morning test we did not chat much on this day maybe it was his plan to build up his suspense for the date. Fast forward to Thursday I'm panicking calling on my friends for support. I'm also excited to be having butterflies in my stomach again. My friend came early I guess because she also wanted to see the guy.

He came, and there he was looking as handsome as he was on Tuesday, dressed formal. I started feeling under dressed cause I did not want to over impress. I got in his car (notice I said I got in his car, I got excited by this because he had his own car meaning he won't stress me about my car hahahaha). We drove to news cafe not so far from where I stayed. I really thought we would go to some fancy restaurant, but news cafe was fine, I guess. We had a great time he told me about himself and that he was from Limpopo and had been staying in Centurion for over 7 years. As the night was going guy kept ordering drinks for me as if his intention was to get me drunk. Well, it worked the night was a vibe and I hadn't drunk like that in a while. I was just determined to have fun. I tell him I think I've had enough it was time to call it quits before I embarrass myself not that I ever get to that drunk stage anyways but didn't want to find out on that night if it was possible. He pays and we go. I seriously had a good time, guy had stories for days I had stories for days, so the date was a success.

We get to my place he goes to the boot and takes out a bottle of wine and gives it to me. I thought it was going to be like in the movies will get a hug and kiss goodbye but NO.

*Remember my last relationship is my only reference for new date or love, we met at our university residence there was no dropping you off after dinner. We rode the bus back home after our lunch at steers and I made him eat ice cream without him telling me he was lactose intolerant. He was sick all the way from town to res. By the time we got to res it was "sharp sharp" as he rushed to his room. I guess to relieve himself that ice cream was a lot. But anyways back to this story.*

I took the wine gave him a hug and said thank you for a great evening. He was like are you not going to invite me in for tea or coffee. I'm like ok come in but we are not drinking this wine have to go to work tomorrow. I was preparing to go make him coffee he says wait come sit with me on the couch first. Now he was very touchy and I'm not saying no it was feeling really good, I mean it's been 3 years in fact more than that cause these touches were new and came with butterflies. I sat down and we were all over each other, his hands, lips everything felt like I'm in a dream. One thing led to another we were in my bed about to do the things I never thought we will do on our first date. I stopped him and he said don't worry I have condoms. I slept with him just like that, he came too quick, and he was not Limpopo sided as per the rumour was out there about guys from that side of the province hahahahaha. It was really not a wonderful experience, but I guess I was just happy with the experience. He quickly got up to dress up and leave. I asked him what's the rush he says, "remember we have work tomorrow we will have plenty of time for more of this". I walk him to the door he kissed me and left so quickly I was a bit shocked but then again, I was too high on alcohol and love to even think much of it.

Relationships with strings attached

The next day no morning text from him, nothing. My friend came early to drop the kids before work she was too excited and said after work, I'm here I want all the tea. She doesn't know I'm starting to regret last night but I give her a huge smile and thank her for taking care of my kids. The whole day went passed and ended no message from him. I decided to send him something "hi guess your day was busy as mine, hope to hear from you soon". I really didn't know what I was saying but I guess now I was talking from emotions of attachment we all know women we are weak when it comes to sex, men do it for fun we do it and get attached. Anyways my message was not even read and no response. My friend came over carrying pizza for us and the kids. I told her the story as we drank the wine that he bought me.

Well, I went to bed still no word from him. Next morning, he finally texts and apologizes for the silence he had issues with his phone. I was relieved, as I was starting to feel like I was 2-night standed if there is such a word hahaha. He tells me he is going to Limpopo and might be offline for a while but as soon as he is back, he will call me. I didn't have a problem with that I had stuff to do for my agency anyways. Tuesday he was back with a bang sending non-stop messages and asking to come visit, offering to even bring food I must just relax and not cook. I told him if my friend can look after the kids no problem otherwise rain check. I phone Sindi she agrees to take the kids. Later he comes carrying food and gifts for the kids as well.

Again, today ended in that quick session in my bed and again immediately after he was done, he dressed up and left. Ghosted me until the next time he will wake me up with a "hey babe I missed you hope you good" this was after I talked to myself for a while on his chat line (the young and naïve me learned the hard way unfortunately, never again did I do this crazy thing of talking to myself on someone's WhatsApp hahahaha). Like a fool every time I fell for his come back to life experiences the sex was not even that good, but I let this go on for a good 2 months. Sometimes we would bump into each other at Park station, and he would pretend to be in such a hurry. Somehow, I was not really bothered because I was starting to suspect he was married, and I was just his sleeping pill when he can't get it from wife. One time my friend was late to get the kids, so they saw him coming inside the house. At that stage I think that's where I woke up from the trans because I never wanted my kids to see me with another man unless it's serious.

This time he came during the day, and it was starting to feel like he is getting comfortable with our on and off thing because now he was telling me how he can help me pay for my place. I declined that offer. I was not struggling to pay, and I was not about to be bought by a man for my silence or that's what I thought in my head. He would then just ask me random questions that suggested he was having issues at home. Like one time he asked me why you woman don't have a problem when your mothers come to visit but if our moms come it's a problem. I did not have an answer for that because I have never been married nor have had an in-law want to sleep over at my place. But I guess him seeing my kids triggered something in me that even when he ghosted me for 2 weeks I didn't care. I did not even send him any messages. After 2 weeks I was woken up by "Hey babe" I got so upset and just muted his chat. It was muted for weeks, and the time I decided to check it I found him talking to himself. I got upset and ended up blocking him. The times we bumped into each other he was now the one looking for my attention. I would smile and pretend to be happy to see him but deep down, I was crying because of how he played with my emotions.

That chapter closed, but now, unfortunately it had opened a space of I need a companion. The space was so wide that I thought of it every day. It didn't help that my friend was also not so lucky in that department, so it became our focus and main conversation. Looking back, I would not have given the thought of having a relationship so much power over my life. Well now my focus was more on my growing agency, the partnerships and friendships I was making.

## Relationships with strings attached

Right when I thought I was done with men, another one came to test me in my weakest state. I was still wounded by the 2 months of on and off "hey babe" relationship. I met this guy when I was planning another event for my agency. Because he also wanted us to be anonymous, I won't give him a name or character just that he was "man anony" (short for anonymous). Well, this guy all I can about him is that he was different, a complete opposite to Volti, in terms of looks, career, education and general being. But he managed to convince me that we should keep our relations secret since he is in the media industry. I agreed, this was the most toxic experience, and it lasted a year and a half. Some days were good some were extremely bad. Man anony, broke up with me on New Year's Eve can you imagine, because I sent him a WhatsApp message saying, "I miss you". I was so hurt and the fact that he was anonymous meaning can't even talk to my mom or sisters about this break up was the worst. While I was still in bed stressed. I get a text from my high school friend Lwandle that I must come to her house for new year's celebration, her mom bought lots of meat and alcohol so we will just braai by her house and catch up. I invited my cousin who then invited his girlfriend it was a welcomed excuse to forget about this crazy break up with man anony. For the first time since I was born, I decided to go have new year's celebration with other people and not my family. My family was shocked, but mom did not stress in fact she said you better sleep there because it won't be safe driving back home after 12 midnight people will be too drunk. The three of us got to Lwandle's place and it was a vibe. The braai was already going on, music was playing loud, we had a good time you would swear I was not just dumped. We were all sitting by the braai area having a good time drinking eating and dancing. I remember the famous song that time was midnight starring so my friend and I were dancing as if we were Busiswa and Moonchild. Every time we would repeat the song it was the best distraction. 12 o'clock struck, me being me I called man anony and he was so happy and acted like he never dumped me, somehow that turned me off. I dropped the call and decided to have fun.

## Relationships with strings attached

My friends' brother received a message that there is another crazy house party full of cool young people that are not from Ladysmith and were just spending money like crazy. My cousin and his girl said they were going to sleep. Me that time I was like it's the first time ever in my life spending new year's outside of home, I'm taking this opportunity let's go. Oh, and this year I was turning 35 mind you Hahaha the Joys of not being married. Ok we went to this party; it was in a very nice suburb in Ladysmith that I never even knew about, and this is my hometown. We saw nice cars parked outside we were also in a nice car. My friend's brother gives a disclaimer before we go out, he says "guys you know I was invited by my age mates right, under 30's so you might be the only old people there besides the couple that owns the house". My friend laughed and gave me lipstick athi syabangenake thina bo yellow bone (we are entering them as yellow bones hahahaha) that don't even need make up. We got there yoh its lit kumnandi yey (it's a vibe). They were still preparing more fireworks, so it was like another countdown all over again. They were younger than us but were playing our type of old school music, so we were right at home. They welcomed us with drinks and snacks, offered us food and we were like no snacks are fine. There was hubbly there as well. I had recently discovered hubbly in my old age, and I was so happy. All of a sudden, the girls were uneasy around us because we were too free. My friend and I laughed because we were clearly way much older than these girls that were worried about us.

While I was busy with my hubbly this guy came and asked me to dance with him. I remember the song that was playing was step in the name of love by R Kelly, remember I told you this party was playing music for the born in the 80's and 90's. I try and refuse and say I can't dance because I could see one girl giving me the side eye. He grabs my hand and says I'll teach you. There we were on the porch dancing away if you know this song you know it's a vibe especially when R Kelly starts instructing us to step side to side. After the dance we went back to the hubbly, and his friends came to join us. Now it's like all of a sudden

## Relationships with strings attached

attention was on us. They ask me where I'm from because they have been coming to Ladysmith and never bumped into me. I was like this is home, but I stay in Centurion now guy dancer gets too excited and says wow I'm staying in Randburg how are you going back we should go together. Well, I tell him that I'm driving back. He got more excited and suggested we should drive back together because he came by plane as he came for the baptism of his friend's daughter. So, he did not want to drive to Ladysmith and Back alone so opted for flights to Pietermaritzburg which meant a shorter driving distance to Drakensburg where the ceremony was held. I looked at this guy and he was extremely dark, handsome, but extremely dark. His face just looked like I've known him for years, he also had an American accent. At some point I hear him speaking French to his friends, so I asked him if they were Congolese, and he says nah we are from Ghana we just like speaking French sometimes. At this stage the girl that was giving me the side eye was looking like she is about to die. I tell the guy it was nice talking to you, but I think it's time you go back to your girlfriend before she kills me for no reason. He laughed so loud and said "ahh this one they have been trying to hook me up with her the whole night but seriously look at her and look us there is no match". I brushed his response off and told him dude go be with your woman.

I carry on having fun with my friend, but she was starting to get tired now, old age creeping in. I show her brother ukuthi ngeke kuyamosheka (old age was catching up with her) she is falling asleep now. The brother says let me take her back home I'm coming then we go to another place they were having a festival we will be there till morning. They left and I stayed with Mr Ghana, conversation was flowing. Now the other girl comes and joins us with her friend I guess to establish what's happening only to find we are just talking about stupid random stuff. My friend's brother quickly came back, and it was time for us to go to the festival. Mr Ghana asks that I go with him, but I told him I came with Sanele (my friend's brother) let's rather meet there.

## Relationships with strings attached

Because he wanted to make a statement, he drove his avis car alone and left the "supposed hook up girl disappointed as he drove off". She then went to another friend's car, I was driving Sanele's car, and we all went to the festival. When we got there, brother was there by my hip asking me what do I want to drink. At this stage I'm all drinked out I just want to dance.

When I want to go to the toilet, he is there like a bodyguard. Side eye girl finally gets courage to come and ask me if we are together. I tell her no I just met this guy today and we are just talking not even relationship related talk. She was like since he came yesterday, she has been trying to get with him she thought today was the day then I came. I was like sorry girl I just came to have fun not get a man, but you can see for yourself he is the one following me everywhere. It was now morning I tell Sanele that I guess we should go now. He says I thought you are going with brother Ghana. I laughed and said let's go home man, there is nothing between me and Mr Ghana we were just having a good time. I tell Mr Ghana that we are going he begs for my number I give him, and we go. I didn't know that I was opening another big can of tinned fish by giving him my number but we came to this earth to learn right?

The next morning, I drove back home, started by picking up my cousin and his girlfriend where they were sleeping. As we drove home, I was just worried about my car as it was starting to give me problems, but luckily, we managed to get home with no problems. I went straight to bed as I was really tired. At around 12:00pm I get a message from Mr Ghana. He was so sweet and wanted to find out if I was home safe. We started talking none stop about any and everything. He even started giving me advise on how to fix my car. Talking to him really made me forget about man anony and I appreciate him for that. The next day I had to go do errands for my mom, so I asked my cousin to go with me. When we were busy shopping, I got a message from Mr Ghana asking me if he can take me out. I told him I am only in town for a few hours then going back home so if he wanted to see me, we could make some time after shopping. He agreed and then we met after shopping. He came with his friend because I told him I am with my cousin. We had a great time once again that we even forgot about time and ended up going back home very late. It helped that my cousin was there because in my moms' eyes I was still a baby even though I was turning 35 that year. My cousin was impressed by the guy because he was intelligent, sweet and spent so much money on us to the point that my cousin could not drive anymore I had to drive us home (he was a permanent resident at the bar). I was happy with him as well but did not want it to be a relationship until we went back to Gauteng, I guess. He was a good man with manners, 2 years younger than me. He liked buying me things. The few times we met while at home he would bring me something.

We ended up not going to Gauteng together. But as soon as we were both in Gauteng, he asked me out on a proper date now just me and him. I told him it would have to be during the day as my helper could only look after the kids during the day. He came to pick me up for our date. I was so excited as he was a sweet and caring man. Also, he was an engineer with big dreams so that was a welcome change from what I had experienced before. Like always when he came to pick me up, he came carrying a box full of sweets, chips and fruits for the kids. This started to be a norm for him every-time he came to pick me up he would bring groceries. The fruits were always there, and they were so delicious that I would look forward to them every time he would come pick me up. In a space of a month, we had seen each other almost every other day. He could not get his hands off me even in public, he would hold my hand steal kisses on the forehead every time we would be waiting on the line at the grocery till or he would just stop me as we walked just to kiss me. I really really enjoyed the attention. He never wanted me to drive so every outing we had he would come pick me up and if I drove to his place, we would park my car and go out in his car. We went on dates, game drives, walks, shopping even went to the gym together that is how close we started getting and I was really starting to fall in love. One time he asked me if he can take me to Menlyn Mall to buy me lingerie, I said yes of course. We went to this other boutique, and he bought the most expensive pieces, in my head I was like I could get used to this. Felt like I had been missing out on being loved right, here was a foreign guy doing all the right things. After shopping for my lingerie, we passed this other boutique he wanted to get in and check out some formal shoes. The shoes he picked were too fancy and expensive to be worn at work every day, besides he was a civil engineer I did not picture him wearing such formal shoes to work. So, I made a joke that - is he getting married why is he buying such a nice shoe. He laughed it off and said it's for Church. I believed him because he loved going to church and had invited me to go with him, but I was going to our local church with the kids. But after the marriage remark it's like it triggered something in him. The next day he told me he was sick and went to the doctor. I asked to come see him he said no he will drink medication and be fine. Later, that night he called me to say he was outside my house. I was surprised because this person was on medication. I went to him; he showed me his doctors note and medication. He was on meds to lower his blood pressure. That's when he dropped the bomb on me that he was really falling in love with me but it's killing him every day that he has a girlfriend back home. There are plans for his family to go to the girlfriends' house and officially announce their relationship (apparently that is what happens in Ghana as part of their culture). My heart sank as well because I was starting to fall for him but appreciated that he was so honest with me. He went on to say he wished he met me sooner before this family meet up was arranged, he could have stopped it but now the plans are too far deep, and his family has been nagging him about him getting old and not having a serious relationship (I didn't know if he was pulling the famous married guys line or was he genuine). We ended things that day because I was not about to be in a confused relation or be the reason another woman was unhappy. Although, it still did not make sense, this guy was posting me everywhere not even once did I suspect that

## Relationships with strings attached

there was something amiss except for the fancy shoes and he was buying a lot of alcohol whereas he did not drink and he would say he was buying it for his uncles for when he goes back home, now I knew it was for the ceremony. Few days later he came again begging me to not let him go he will talk to his family that he no longer wants to be with the girl as he was going home in 2 weeks-time. Silly me said yes, but it was no longer the same because I knew there was another girl in the picture. The day came for him to go home, I offered to drive him to the airport, but he said he did not want to stress me he will take an uber there. The first few days he was home we spoke every day; he was buying me things and showing me that he will bring them for me. Things like traditional cloths and jewellery. He kept talking about going to another area to buy me something really special. I was ok but like I said things were never the same. He then went offline for some time citing being busy, so I gave him that space and I was not about to be talking to myself on his WhatsApp like I did with that other Limpopo guy.

One day my friend suggested we go see a medium because people at her work have been raving about how accurate she was. I had never consulted a medium or sangoma or anything of that sort but was curious. I had just recently heard about mediums through a reading by one lady that was visiting Metro FM. I was then curious and convinced myself it's not against my religion because she talks to angels. We made an appointment, and I only wanted to know why I am not getting another job after so many years of looking. When my appointment came it was so different nothing that I had ever seen or experienced before. Immediately when I walked in the lady mentioned that I was so lucky I already came with my ancestors that are watching over me, in fact they are excited to see me or talk to me. The reading started immediately as she said my ancestors and angels were eager to speak to me, not much was said about my work, but she insisted on telling me about my relationship future. She said a lot of things even describing the man I was to marry. I was just sitting there looking at this white lady with shock. I then decided to ask her about this Ghana guy that I am dating. She was like you guys are soul mates and have amazing chemistry (she was right about the chemistry I was a bit sceptical about the soul mates' part). She went on to say but I should know that the guy is about to get married even though he loves me a lot, he even wants to back out of the marriage because of me but he respects his family too much that he will never go against their wishes to see him married to this girl. My jaw dropped; he was getting married not just a family meet up!!! She went on to say without a doubt this guy loves me and he has been planning in his head how he will make this work and he has been wanting to be close to my kids but I must be warned he will never be in the relationship fully because he is getting married soon, even though he is so strongly drawn to me he is a man that respects his family and culture too much. His family would never accept me and that would break him so much because unfortunately his family will always come first to him. Right now, his family loves the woman he is about to marry, although he is having second thoughts, he will never leave her because he would never want to disappoint his family especially his father. In his head he is thinking like he can do like his uncle and have a wife in Ghana and in South Africa but that won't be good for me in the long run because his family will not accept me. In my head I was like I would never agree to be in a polygamous relationship anyways, I was thinking his family would not accept me because I have kids (these were thoughts in my head, and they were pouring water into my self-doubt tree that was growing every day). I was so shocked but somehow, I knew from the shoes to the alcohol and confession something was just off. The medium told me to peacefully let him go someone that was meant for me was on the way and I will not have any doubts about him. (Well, I have been looking for that man since 2018 haahahahaha akafiki!!!)

That weekend I decided to search for him on Facebook something I had never thought of doing because he said he was not active on social media. He was right his page was like a ghost page, he last updated something when he was still in university.

## Relationships with strings attached

There was a photo of him and a girl from their tertiary days. Then I remember he said he met his girlfriend when they were studying at UCT. She moved back home, and he got a job in Johannesburg. I went to the comments on the photo, and I saw his friend that was with him in Ladysmith when we met. When I get to the friends' page, there are photos of him attending Mr Ghana's wedding!!!! There were so many congratulations on the comments section and one of the comments was a thank you from the bride, nothing from Mr Ghana. So, I went to the bride's page and that's where I saw all her wedding pics. It was a beautiful beach wedding, she looked really gorgeous. I was not even jealous after seeing the pictures and how happy they were. The pictures were still new meaning the wedding was either on the day or day before. There was Ghana wearing the shoes we picked that day he denied that they were for a wedding. I think God prepared me for this shock by me suspecting (intuition!) and getting to hear from the medium before I could see it myself. I decided that day that I am stepping back from whatever was happening between us.

The day of his return came. He was calling me so happy saying he cannot wait to see me; he bought me everything he wanted to buy me. I just responded like a zombie no emotions or reactions. I did not even know how I could talk to him so calmly. Immediately when he landed at OR Tambo International Airport, he told me he was going to his place to get his car and come see me, he couldn't wait to see me and to give me my gifts. I just snapped out of zombie mode and told him he should rather give the gifts to his wife. He went dead silent, then started apologising. I stopped him and told him its ok no need to apologise because he had told me about the woman although he failed to tell me they were getting married; it hurts but I was fine. Deep down I was really fine, disappointed yes, but I had experienced a refreshingly different kind of love with him that I could not even hate him, but I could not continue with the relationship anymore.

Relationships with strings attached

I sometimes ask myself what his plan was because he was so excited to see me like he did not just get married. Like always, I told my friends about this, there is one particular one that always reminds me of this phase in my life like I deliberately chose someone who was going to get married while we were together. Every time she goes through something low, she would make herself feel better by saying "ehh Brenda remember you once saw your man getting married to another woman on Facebook". This used to hurt me, and I asked myself why can't I keep my experiences to myself, because they are now being used as a joke against me. But not sharing my experiences would not be good for me I guess, right now I am sharing my life with whoever that's going to read my book. I had to learn to let go of the pain of being laughed at, which was more painful than the actual act. Now I can laugh at myself and say "yah Brenda, you made it to the statistics girl. The one they always joke about when the big holidays are approaching hahahaha. You literally found out about your man's marriage on social media never mind that a Medium also warned you about his upcoming nuptial you still made it to the statistics".

I named this chapter the start of my self-doubt because at this stage I was starting to think I really don't have this life thing under control. I was starting to base my life on finding the perfect partner that I was now no longer in touch with what was happening around me. I had business ideas, and I could start them, but they were not making any money. Maybe it was because of my heart and soul was just too vested in finding a partner. I was determined to not fail in this field otherwise I would have given my kids a broken home foundation. I did not want that. Even though my mom always assured me that it's not failing to raise my kids alone, I was starting to doubt my life decisions. Because I was still hurt from the fact that I had just found an ideal man, a man that was determined to take care of me from the beginning right to the end. I never even spent one cent when I was with him. He was a provider that also loved cooking for me and making future plans that I was so sure we will end up growing old together, only to find it was a two-month fantasy, he was planning a future with me but had a reality with another woman. I was determined to forget about him as quick as possible, seeing him check my status updated was giving me heart palpitations every time. I ended up blocking and deleting his number. It was at this stage that I started noticing that there are two guys always commenting on my WhatsApp status updates. I had a fashion show coming up later in the year, so I was advertising it on my status almost every day and I was also posting my normal crazy updates. My phone since I started the agency had many numbers some from call outs for adverts, others from people I have worked with and models. Any given status would have more than 100 views that's how busy my phone was. So, there were these particular guys that were consisted in talking to me and I started entertaining them because I needed a distraction. I did not want to cry over this past relationship, nor did I want to miss the guy. The distractions worked. One of the guys we met through my other event he supplied me with two great artists. We also followed each other on Facebook so I knew he was in a relationship, and he always posted nice messages about his woman, so I knew our talk was what it was just purely jokes and business. More about him on the following chapter.

The second guy was just straight up asking me out. Every day he would send sweet messages and memes. He was good looking but looked a bit young. So, I would brush him off by saying his too young for me. He persisted until one day I said fine let's meet. Did we not meet at KFC!!! hahahahaha (Lord I just had flash backs). I was meeting another potential client in Pretoria CBD, so he suggested that we meet after my meeting. I thought we would probably go to the restaurant at the State Theatre or something since he insisted, I park there. He came to get me at the parking lot, my goodness this guy was nothing like his pictures and messages he was sending. His aura was just vibrating too low, felt like he was now intimidated by me. He even looked a bit gay something was not right about him, but I

## Relationships with strings attached

was already here and interested in seeing where the day would end. We walked to another centre nearby and we walked into KFC. I could not believe it but stayed calm. I just ordered a milk shake, we talked he was still the guy that was full of jokes on WhatsApp just that his photos were heavily photoshopped and his gay hand gestures were popping up more and more. He then felt the need to tell me that he is not gay, but people think he is. He was nearly raped by a guy in Cape Town. But yah that was a complete disaster however me being me and also vibrating low I did not cut conversations with him; we ended up being friends. He wanted to be an actor so I would suggest auditions for him etc. He had a talent management agency which was not doing so good, now I remember that's how I got his number. He was in another group I was in, that had a lot of Talent Managers and people in the media industry. I started helping him fix his business page and it started growing. He messed up by now trying to steal my clients and the last draw was when he started dating one of my models and convinced her to leave me after I got her a paying gig. Paying gigs were few and almost non-existent for my agency and the one paying client he decided to pull a crazy stunt. I ended our friendship immediately. It was a great two- or three-months distraction. I had forgotten about Mr Ghana and was planning my fashion show which was looking like it was going to be a big success. Guy number two was helping me with venue selection etc. Things changed with him when he asked me out for a coffee date, but wait he deserves a whole chapter or two so more about him in the next chapter.

# PARTNER BETRAYAL TRAUMA

*"First coined by psychologist Jennifer Freyd, betrayal trauma occurs when a person's trust is violated by a person or system that they rely on for survival. In other words, when you trust a person or institution to provide for you physically, mentally, and/or emotionally, and they aren't able to do so or if they end up harming you instead, this can have a significant and lasting impact.*

***Partner Betrayal Trauma*** *is when the perpetrator is a significant other, such as a boyfriend / girlfriend or spouse. It is entirely possible in fact, it's relatively common for an individual to be reliant in some way on a partner, or to trust that they will meet the other's needs. These needs might be financial (paying bills, managing funds), emotional (intimacy, support) or physical (sex, safety, basic needs).*

*To betray that trust might look like cheating, manipulation, physical / sexual / emotional abuse or withholding / misusing financial resources. In some cases, a person might not even be entirely reliant on their partner – at least not literally – but it still feels as though leaving the perpetrator is not an option.*

*Regardless of how or in what way a person is reliant on a partner, when the perpetrator betrays the victim's trust it can leave a lasting mark. Say a person was happily married for 20 years. They shared everything with the spouse, including a home and children, and relied on the spouse to provide a stable, loving relationship. If they suddenly learned that their spouse was cheating on them, how might that affect them?"* (Quoted from www.psychologytoday.com)

## Relationships with strings attached

If you also look at it from a spiritual standpoint, your soul can be shattered, fragmented and broken. This happens through trauma, and it can be repeated instances of trauma, death of a loved one and also dabbling in the practices that are outside religion. When the door is open through these experiences then your soul can be held captive.

The soul can also cleave to another person i.e Sexual attachment (sex outside marriage worse you have it with multiple partners meaning you leave a piece of you in all those partners).

Finding healing after this kind of trauma is a really long journey. I had to add this extract because it explains exactly what I went through in the relationship that I entered into in the next chapter. However, the understanding that one needs to know, is that your soul can be healed through the blood of Jesus Christ (more about this in my next book).

# CHAPTER 6

# RED FLAGS

What are red flags in a relationship?

Physical, emotional, and mental abuse are undeniable red flags in any relationship. Physical abuse is easier to pick up. But emotional and mental abuse can be just as damaging in the long run. And just like physical abuse, mental and emotional abuse can cause PTSD (post-traumatic stress disorder).

I ignored the red flags in the beginning in fact I covered them up, ok reflect with me.

I remember when I started dating guy number 2. I started looking for his profiles on all social media as well as the internet. Something we normally did with my friends when we had an interest in a guy. I guess it's something anyone does. There was the first red flag!! A cloned page that looked exactly like his page that I've known for over a year, but it had the following words in brackets under his name (Certified Scammer). His bio went on to say beware of this scammer. I started panicking I was like what the hell? What is the meaning of this? Like always what I did I asked him about this page. Like always he laughed it off and actually found it cute that I was looking him up and found that page. His response was, "you see baby I told you I was not the only one stalking you, you also stalking me". I was a little ashamed, but I wanted answers. "No guy answer me are you planning to scam me too?". He laughed again and said, "no man this guy was just jealous of me, we had a little misunderstanding, and he decided to open that page". I was really getting worried because his responses were too chilled. I asked him "So where did he get all your details certificates and ID copies?". He replied, "I was using his laptop since we were staying together so I had a folder with my things on his laptop". I asked him angrily "so why have you not resolved this or removed this page don't you think it looks bad on you to have such things written about you?". He laughed again, "It does not bother me because it's lies. I tried removing it without success so I figured I would just live with it and enjoy the fame." Well, it bothered me I could not be having a man I'm in love with having such a degrading profile.

Now I was alone at home thinking how my friend would find this page and convince me not to continue with him. She had access to doing credit checks which is something she did with her suitors and now I'm thinking his ID copy is there she is going to do it and find things that will end this before it even takes off. Besides I've known this guy for over a year, he is a decent guy I believe his explanation.

I wonder if I really believed him or if I just desperately wanted this relationship to be the one. Heck, I prayed and prayed even had a long crying spree on the N1 highway driving back home from work. I remember I was passing Midrand and crying like a baby asking God why is he not sending me my husband he knows I value family and cannot carry on attracting people who just want to use me and leave. At the end of the prayer, I was like the next guy I date will be my forever no matter what. Now here was my forever having a reputation of being a scammer!!! No way this cannot be right. I woke up in the middle of the night and had this epiphany that no man let me just report this page as a fake account or something like that. I don't remember really what I reported it under but the next day the page was gone. He called me to thank me, telling me that he got

## Relationships with strings attached

the message that I reported that page and it has been removed. He was so grateful because he tried to do it before with no success. I found it strange he was not successful in removing it because it was so easy to do.

Anyway, I was now happy that the page was no longer there. Anyone can Google him now I'm good. (Wow Brenda waze wazifaka ku trap and God as well as your guardian angels were warning you so very early before you got attached but no this was your, forever, right?). So now I had few questions on his main account, but I chose to keep them to myself before he really thinks I'm stalking him. Remember in the previous chapter I said I knew him for a year before we dated. Not really knew him but we were Facebook friends for a little over a year and the previous year we met when he supplied one of my events with 2 artists that he was "managing". So, we would occasionally talk on WhatsApp, and he was always there liking and commenting on my Facebook page so that's how we knew each other.

He liked sharing his girlfriend and writing sweet messages to her and she would also respond with sweet messages so I never really saw us being a couple our interaction was purely business, and he would sometimes offer to be my personal trainer as I used to joke a lot that I need to get back in shape. One time before the sparks lit, he did a whole workout routine and eating plan for me. That is when I realised, I was talking to this guy every day now; morning and night and our conversations were good. Earlier that year he had posted a photo of a baby and tagged his girlfriend but when I went to his page this post was no longer there along with those lovey-dovey posts, he was sharing about his girl maybe 1 or 2 was left but it was not as explicit as the ones he deleted. So, one day he posted he is done with love he tried but every time he is used. The comments were dodgy I remember his best friend, the guy that I booked for my event, he commented and said, "my guy you need to stop playing with girls, nigga you could be far in life if you could just focus and stop with this girl shit". Other comments were along those lines, but they were not as blunt. So, I was like is that why he

## Relationships with strings attached

deleted all those posts? Anyways I never asked him I just waited to see where this was going. He liked posting his baby girl a lot. I asked him how many kids he have, he said one (the baby girl that he liked posting). I was surprised because early this year he posted a picture of a newborn boy and even captioned it "proud parents" while tagging his girlfriend. There were lots of congratulations on the post with him and the girl responding yet now he is saying he is having one child which is this girl that he always posts, and she was much older 4/5 years old. I asked him again He said yah man I only have 1 kid.

Now his posts were different our conversations were different as well. I started telling my friends about him and everyone was saying go for him, but I would tell my one friend that no man something is just offish about this guy, but I can't put my figure on it. She would be like you deserve happiness girl go for him. If you can check, how many red flags did I spot but completely ignored until I agreed to us going on a breakfast date? The breakfast date was the sweetest and romantic thing I had ever experienced I was head over heels from that day. I remember I had a business meeting at SABC Park that day, I was so happy even told the people there that I'm from the sweetest first date ever. I was happy, scratch that, I was over the moon. We were inseparable from that day, he was my wake-up call, when I get to work call, and my goodnight call daily. His voice would just melt me every time he called. The following Sunday we were supposed to have date number two at his place, he was cooking lunch for me. It felt like Sunday was a lifetime away. I got an invite to attend a business friend's birthday on Saturday, so I decided to ask him to attend with me. I just needed an excuse to see him more than once. Saturday came he came to my place looking good, we drove to the party in my car, we looked good, and it was the perfect first outing as a couple and mind you we had not kissed yet so today was the day we had to have that kiss before we got to the venue. The venue was not that far from my place, so it was a short drive. I forgot to mention he was a door opener from day one, he never wanted me to open my own door for as long as we travelled together. This went on throughout our relationship. I was uncomfortable at first until I got used to the special treatment. Anyway, we got to the party it was great. His eyes were on me the whole time until one lady commented that you are so lucky to have someone who adores you so much. The party host was getting married in a few months' time, so she gave us an invite to her wedding which was going to be in KZN at some beautiful lodge. I was like wow this is really happening I'm having a plus 1 now for invites.

The night was amazing except for some smallanyana (small) red flags again. He insisted we move upstairs to the bar and carry on the party there. He said we must order drinks, everyone figured dude is paying. We had fun drank and danced. He kept going out saying his sorting out something at the garage. He came back now everyone wanted to leave and there was already an argument about who is going to pay. He did not entertain the argument in fact at some stage I think he hinted I should pay half for our drinks because he couldn't find his card. I was like no way I did not plan on spending money today. So, I ignored the suggestions until some guy offered to pay for all of us as he was asking one of the girls out. I couldn't believe what just happened but quickly forgot when he whispered nawe (even you) next year uzobe uthi (will be saying) my husband is waiting for me at home. As most of the ladies were saying that as the time to leave came. He offered to drive us back home that night. His driving was a bit questionable, but I was in love and could not wait to get home and get it on, the kids will be sleeping they won't even see him in the morning he is going to work first thing, so they won't see him leave also. The night ended passionately, and the morning was glorious. I was happy even had first time experience of wetting the bed he was that magical which is why I think I held on so long I guess I was in love and dickmatised. I dropped him off at the taxis and he promised to cook me a very special meal, remember we had a lunch date. I got home on cloud 9 again. Told my 2 friends about the

## Relationships with strings attached

experience we were all so happy. The next thing I saw on his page was that he changed his relationship status to "in a relationship" The congratulations came flooding in. I was finished, thanking God for answering my prayers.

I went to his place; it was a shared flat with a roommate he was not talking to I found that strange even the energy between the two of them was not good. The guy looked like a decent guy, but he had nothing good to say about him in fact he did not even want me to greet him. In hindsight, I'm thinking was it because he stayed with another woman there and he did not want me to find out because it was not necessary how he was treating him (another red flag ignored). Lunch came he had the table set up everything was beautiful and well thought out. The food was delicious it was my favourite (chicken Condon blue). This must be a sure sign indeed that my forever is here. Everything was perfect, the food, the conversation, the music, the pampering, I was in heaven. We could not keep our hands off each other and had a few steamy episodes until I said no, I must leave don't want to drive at night in an area I don't know. He had driven my car a few times now to the shops, to help me park and he offered to drive me to Sunnyside as he was going to meet a friend there at least I wouldn't stress about driving in an unknown area. When we got to the friend's place, he wanted me to meet the friend I was happy to meet his friend and the energy there was way much better than the roommate's energy, so I quickly took his side then painted the roommate as the bad guy.

The next day he told me, he had to go somewhere for a month to fix the wrong things he did in a rural area in Limpopo. He wants to start afresh in life, and he does not want those things to come back to haunt him and mess up our relationship he is planning to do the right thing with me, I'm his for life. I was already attached a month felt like forever, but he was calling and messaging me every day assuring me that when he came back it's me and him for life. I didn't know that him saying that meant he was going to move in with me because immediately when he came back, he came to my place. Slept over and in the morning offered to drive me to the gautrain. He did not want me to stress about walking a long distance from the parking to the train. He was not back at work, so he offered to fix a few things in the house that he saw needed fixing and he would come get me after work. I agreed but was a bit sceptical. But that quickly went out the window when he got out opened my door and walked me into the station carrying my laptop bag holding my hand. He gave me a long hug and kiss as I left to go to the train. Yeyi I was smiling all the way from Centurion to Park Station. When I got to the office, I sent him a message as he asked me to. When I opened my bag to take out my laptop there was a lunchbox already packed for me. I was sold and gone same time from that day I knew I was 100% hooked.

He later picked me up from the station. When I got home there were boxes of Jack Daniel's in the garage. I was like wait a minute so much alcohol he laughed and said nah man those are the only boxes I could get for my things. Things!!! Did I hear correctly? We got in the house it was so clean at this stage I did not have a full-time helper anymore because the kids were old and was trying to save to be able to get back to buying property again since I had to sell my old place. I get to my room he had already re-arranged and got himself a section in my cupboard and his clothes were there. Haibo; the dude moved in while I was at work. I don't know if I was happy or not, but I got in the flow and just like that, we were an official couple living together. My son Tiro was really happy about this because he was longing for a father figure, and they got along very well but Angela took very long to adjust to the situation. Now that I know all the things that came with this relationship, I wish I did not ignore even the first red flag. I would have saved myself from a whole lot of things that went wrong in my life. But I guess we live to experience and grow from what we learn as we journey along in life.

What I learned is that it's not only God that listens to our prayers the devil was listening and taking notes on that highway passing Midrand because wow a lot of my hurt and false

## Relationships with strings attached

happiness happened in that proximity. The Midrand demons were on full alert hahaha. But the Bible says, *"all things work together for good to those who love God, to those who are the called according to His purpose"* Romans 8:28. Even though the devil was on a plan to destroy me I still came out victorious in everything that happened throughout this relationship. There is more about this encounter in the following chapter.

# CHAPTER 7

# THE FRAUD I MEAN THE FAKE LOVE CONTINUED

Yeah, I know this chapter caught your attention from the cover of the book, but just like the chapter above that birthed all that unfolded in this journey, I had reservations about everything that was happening, but I still let it happen in my life. I am not sure if it was desperation for marriage or was it that I was under a spell, but the things I went through, with this man do not make sense. As I mentioned above guy moved himself into the house so literally, I was in an unplanned "vat n sit". As uncomfortable as everything was, I still did not stop it but again went with the flow. I don't know where to start but all I can say a lot happened in this relationship so much, so I feel like I met the devil himself on the day that I met this guy. Sometimes I would have random days where I would ask him "Why are you allowing the devil to use you?" I don't know where those words came from, but I just knew my spirit was crying out for my safety it took me a long time to really listen to the cry.

Anyway, let me try and paint a picture of this relationship even though putting it in one chapter would not do justice to it but I will try. We were now living in my house as a "happy couple" with my two kids. In the beginning, it was not so bad after I got over the shock of him moving in uninvited. I think he was strategic in his move because he moved in after he had disappeared for a month citing, he was fixing his life so that when he came back, he wouldn't have any burdens following him. He was to settle down with me and start a new life. I guess my heart was so excited that someone was talking settling down with me that I completely forgot about the red flags and the shock of him moving in. It became a norm that he would wake up early in the morning to make breakfast for all of us as well as making lunchboxes. My daughter used school transport so she would be the first one to leave the house then we would go with my son as he would first drop him at the creche and then drop me at the Gautrain station.

He always came up with an excuse of why he was not going to work the excuses were not adding up, but I was starting to warm up to the fact that my load was really getting light. He would clean the house and do the laundry for all of us, he would sometimes involve the kids but at this stage I was not allowed to do anything even taking off my own shoes, he would say I worked too hard he wanted to take care of me, and I should allow him to take care of me. I am not going to lie it was all good. I can say I started falling in love, but the good feelings were about to be short-lived. My cousin had reservations about him. He asked me many times if I was sure about him and if I was not suspicious of how I had never seen his car and what made him move in with me so quickly. I don't even know what I told him I just know it was a crazy story he had spinned on me. My friends were happy, or I thought they were but when things went south, they were the first to say we really did not like him for you. I never appreciated that because they could have saved me but just watched me go down a sinkhole only to tell me after that "we did not like the guy for you". We did not stay together long enough for me to find out he had a really bad short temper and the one that was always on the receiving end of this short temper was my son. He was only 4 years old when he moved in, but he would hit him randomly every time he would get irritated by something that he would do. I mean he was 4 years old he was allowed to be free and explore as he was growing up, but guy would just get irritated and beat him up. If I stepped in, I would be reminded that he is trying to build a bond with him and part of that is to discipline him as a boy and if I stop him, it means I don't trust him to help me raise my kids then why are we in a relationship, how would we get married if I don't trust him with my kids. This truly bothered me, and it never got better instead it was worse, sometimes he would hit him until he got bruised. He would then apologize saying he will do better he was not raised well and it's his upbringing that made him that way. I would try by all means to protect my son whenever he would lose his temper when I am around, but most beatings would now happen when I am not around.

I was now not happy to continue with this relationship but did not have the balls to tell him to leave my house. It was a crazy roller coaster of a relationship 1 day we are fighting the next we are in love. He never used to hit me, but he had ways of manipulating me to take my car or use my money without my consent that would really upset me more especially because I was trying to save to buy a house for my kids. He had this tendency of over-cleaning when he was angry or couldn't sleep which was also very worrying because he literally lived for cleaning and would sometimes involve the kids in his cleaning sprees. One time he decided to pass time by cleaning the top of my cupboard where I kept all my important documents. I am not sure whether he was snooping or cleaning but what upset me is that he decided to throw away a magazine I had saved for memories as it had Angela as a cover baby, and she had her own fashion and playful spread in the middle pages as it was Your Baby magazine. When I asked him about it, he said he was shocked why I am keeping such an old magazine, and he threw it away. He felt no remorse about it in fact he could not believe I was complaining about a magazine I should have been happy that he cleaned my cupboard. This guy had so many things that hurt me, but I still carried on with the relationship. He had no empathy, loved fighting with people even for simple things that it was so painful to even go anywhere with him. He had no regard for other people at all, even his driving felt like being in a war zone because he drove like he owned the road no regard for road signs as well as other drivers. This got us involved in a very bad accident which I know God really saved me from it as I don't know how we got out of it with no scratches. I remember one time my cousin invited us to a party that he was hosting with his wife. My guy fished all the expensive alcohol with no regard for other people. I had never been so embarrassed in my life. I made a conscious decision to not go with him anywhere again. By this time, it was almost 6 months, and we were planning for my fashion show that I normally hosted on my birthday month. The plans for the show went well, he was helping me although he would sometimes inflate some prices of things he would insist on buying himself. Till today I say guy probably has a wife in Zimbabwe or something because guy really really loved money.

Our first real fight started on the day of my fashion show. I had put him in charge of artists since when we met, he was an artist manager as well. He had an artist that was performing on the day, and he was the one that introduced me to the venue owners. On the day he kept on looking worried like he owed someone lots of money. I would ask him what's wrong, he wouldn't say but he was upset that I was not trusting him with giving him the money he wanted. I couldn't give him any money as all my money was used in preparation for the event and did not want to be broke, so I saved other money that I received for online tickets. I was really frustrated about the planning like anyone who is having an event would be. I found them in the venue putting up my main banner in the wrong place and apparently, I did not talk to him nicely and he was grumpy the whole event. I ended up asking one of the photographers to be in charge of artists because now he was moody and trying everything to sabotage the event. I think till today I am scared to plan another fashion show because of the trauma I went through that day. He decided to be in charge of the door a very strategic move for him to get money because I never got a cent from the entrance fees and the place was fully booked. We were never the same after that event. Every time he would remind me of how I disrespected him at my event, he even wanted to leave but he stayed out of respect for my sister. Every time we would have an argument I would be reminded of that day. If I wanted to drive my car I would be reminded of that day. It was just a mess. This went on for some time. He then started driving a random Toyota Yaris and if I asked him about it, he would say it's a friend's car (I later found out it was his very much much older girlfriend's car). I was really starting to be annoyed by everything he did but again never ended this relationship.

This guy had no ID, no talking about his family, the only people that were in his life were his friends. During December holidays I left him with my house and car, the bravest move I have ever made in my whole entire life. During the holidays I was just uneasy. One day I called him he was acting strange. I told him I had a dream he was in an accident he denied it. Then few days later he told me he was visiting his friend in Sunnyside and got an accident. I asked him about the car, and he was upset that I don't even ask about him, but I am worried about the car. How was I to worry about someone who took a whole week to tell me that he was in an accident with my car. Anyways I came back from the December holidays. He came to pick us up from the bus station and the first thing that greeted me was the huge dent on the body of the car. I was so hurt and thinking how I will claim for this from my insurance 2 weeks later, and he never had a driver's license. Again, he was upset that I am only worried about the car. Conversation went back to the event incident. We were literally fighting every day at this point. But in our fights, we were still having sex.

One day I found my garage full of things like a person was moving in again. He told me his friend is looking for a place and, in the meantime, needed a place to keep her things. These things were a lot even brought unwanted guests (cockroaches) I was not happy at all. They stayed for one month in my garage. One evening the woman came to pick up the things, she was driving

## Relationships with strings attached

the very same Yaris that he would drive sometimes. Because she was very old, I didn't think there was a relationship. I had a box full of my CD collection as well as Angela's barbie movie collection. One day when I came back from work, I couldn't see this box. I asked him he brushed it off. I started saying probably the woman took it by mistake he started shouting saying what would she do with CD's till today my heart is sore for my CD's and Angela's things but on that day, I was really emotional even started crying for my things hahahaha. I didn't know that the crying was because I was pregnant. My goodness in less than a year I was now pregnant with this guy's child!!

It was at this point that he started coming clean about his identity. He came home one day and put his passport on my bed and started apologizing for lying to me. When I read his passport, I was not shocked that he was not South African but Zimbabwean. When I met him, I asked him if he was from outside the country because he did not have a local resemblance, he said he was from Limpopo, but his grandfather was Zimbabwean. I guess he did not completely lie about his identity because if his grandfather was Zimbabwean, it meant he also had Zimbabwean blood hahaha. I think at this stage he felt some sense of relief because he knew I was pregnant with his child and now I knew his identity. He started telling me about his real job of working at a restaurant and he wanted to go back since there will be another member of the family we are going to need the money. He was a very good salesperson that one of his clients liked him so much and gave him a job in an insurance company. This was supposed to be a blessing but became a curse. Because we were now fighting about him wanting to use my car to get to work and I must use uber to the Gautrain. Imagine I was pregnant and subjected to use public transport even on days I would have driven straight to work I would be expected to use public transport. I would refuse and drop him at work, and he would complain about me making him late and not supporting his career. Few months in, the employer found out he was not legal in the country, and they had to let him go, he was then back to the restaurant. Now he was going to one far away from our area because he said he didn't want to bump into people that know me and embarrass me. This then meant that the car was working overtime and most of the money he was making was going to petrol. There was no benefit at all in this, he was better off staying at home and cleaning because I was funding the trips to work but there was no return. He started working night shift but most of those shift he would be parked at some complex next to the mall where his restaurant was. I found out while I was in hospital that he was actually visiting a girlfriend he was actually even using her iPhone to take photos of our son's birth.

In all the 9 months of pregnancy I did not want him to touch me or do anything, so we did not have sex for the whole 9 months. I guess my body was just responding to the regret I was feeling of getting pregnant with someone I was not in good terms with. Now my pregnancy was an excuse for him not to marry me also my event incident was another reason he was hesitant to marry me. At this stage I was also not sold on the idea of our forever. I was feeling for my son and couldn't really see raising another son with this short-tempered manipulative man. I finally gave birth, and I nearly died in hospital because it's like after giving birth God wanted me to find out everything about him. I had the craziest dream where I saw all the things he was doing behind my back. I woke up my heart was raising, and I was bleeding so heavily. When I went to the toilet, I nearly fell from being dizzy. I called the nurses and had to have emergency blood transfusion. My health was never back to itself after that. But that was not the worst of it all. The movie was about to begin.

A few months prior, while pregnant the roof of my sitting room caved in. I am not really sure what caused it but when I told my landlord he wanted me to pay for it. We had a huge fight about it until he agreed to fix it but asked me to give him some time because he was financially strapped. I agreed but he took his time until I gave birth. I then decided we have been living in

## Relationships with strings attached

such a place for more than six months I am just going to fix the roof and deduct the money from the rent. I did just that and the landlord was angry. 3 days after coming home from the hospital he came to the house shouting for us to open the gate. I was in my room and guy was watching TV. He got so annoyed that he went outside and beat up the guy. I was not upset about this because I was also angry about the landlord's disrespect, but I think he took it overboard because apparently, he really did do some serious damage. The landlord opened a case against him and later in that evening the police came to get him. He was arrested, now I had to look for a lawyer to help us out because I was never in such a situation and remember he was not legal in the country. My friend referred me to her husband's friend who was a good lawyer. She helped us but at a very high cost. I had to now go into my savings to make sure he does not go to jail. The landlord wanted justice in every way so much so that he even opened a case of theft and vandalism against me saying I stole his satellite dish and horse pipe when I moved out, I also damaged his house which I never did. I even left my own satellite dish in his house. Luckily this case never went anywhere the police quickly saw that it was all a lie.

This was the most draining part of my life, and this relationship was not getting any better. I was now subject to gossip that I even lost a so-called friend who was spreading false rumours about us being on the run from the police. Remember I had just given birth and now I was frequenting courts and police stations with a newborn. This was the worst period of my life, but it was only a tip of what was to come.

Before we moved to a different house, guy had convinced me on a plan that was going to ensure that we are able to get a house since I had used up all my savings that were for the new house deposit. He had met business partners that were going to do business with him that was going to be a success. I believed him because as I said before guy had a smooth tongue, he could sell water to a fish, so I was convinced that him venturing into business was a good idea. I guess I also wanted some relief from the financial burdens I was having, so much so that I wanted this new business venture to work. Since he could not open a bank account as he needed a bank account for his "new business venture" so told me he was thinking of asking a friend to open an account for him. He would ned to keep the account active as a good motivation to his business partners. From time to time, he would need my help to deposit money in the account and he would use the money to pay for things in the house since he does the house errands anyways (at this point I was just a human being living, because he oversaw everything even buying me pads). So, he said with the account he would relieve my cards and use his own card. It didn't make sense at the time he told me, but like all his plans when he told me he was not looking for an opinion or opposition, but it was just a curtesy to let me know that this is how I am going to use you now. Well at the time I didn't have this revelation I just listened and obeyed like a slave listening to her master. It was only a few months in that my mind was opened to what was really happening.

Ok let me go back to where the mind games and scheming began. He firstly convinced me to sell my car (a Dodge Calibre) so that we could buy a BMW that we can call his, so that my family will respect him when he takes me home in December with the new baby. I did that and actually told everyone that the BMW was his car while I was paying the hefty instalment every month. He then convinced one of his artist friends to open an account which he would use under his name saying he will build his credit profile so that they can be able to get a loan to buy studio equipment for him and also pay me back for the savings money that I had used throughout bailing him out on all the court situations that were still going on. Also remember he said it was leverage for his business partners (that is what he told me anyways).

That was the most traumatizing experience, from him getting arrested over and over and having to finally getting community service as a sentence after paying his way through to get that sentence. He now convinced me to sometimes put money into

## Relationships with strings attached

this new account he would be using, and he will take care of the bills. Now suddenly, he started getting loans with this account and I guess this newfound freedom made him feel more like a man because he was a different person. He was never home, driving around with this new BMW and now having a fake salary of over R25 000. He would also make himself fake pay slips using my company name. This went truly out of control that when I found out what was really happening, I started fearing for my job saying I cannot partake in this anymore because this was pure fraud, and I could lose my job if anyone could find out this is what I was exposing myself too. We started fighting now about my money being deposited in this account every month. He would become angry and say he was trying to help me but instead I am being selfish. It was now only two months after moving into our new "rented" home (I truly loved this place it was at a golf estate and reflected exactly the area I wanted to raise my kids in). One day I found a flyer of someone selling avocados knowing how much he loved them I sent him the flyer. Instead of buying avocados he decided to join the business. Imagine doing avocado deliveries with a BMW it did not make any financial sense, but he was a guy you couldn't tell anything or try to reason with him about anything. The avocados were less then R70 but now he started having regular customers in Midrand. We would fight about this delivery, and I would ask him why his business partner is not doing the delivery because he stayed in Tembisa which was much closer to Midrand then us in Centurion. He would be furious saying it was his client and it was not about money but about building his reputation for more customers and building partnerships for the business he was trying to start. In the very same month, he started frequenting Midrand.

For the very first time since I met him this one night he never came home. I was so worried thinking he had an accident I never slept. When I checked on Facebook there was a horrible accident that happened that night involving a BMW, I was so scared. The next morning, I phoned his brother whom I had

## Relationships with strings attached

recently met when he brought him to live with us for 2 months when he was looking for a job in South Africa. He was not familiar with the country as it was his first time coming this side. After talking to his brother, he suddenly reappeared, his phones were now working and came up with a story that he was having business talks in his Nigerian friend's house and police came to arrest all of them. He was in custody and needing money to bribe the police. I couldn't believe how he got himself in trouble with the police after going through such a draining court process which was still not concluded as he was still doing community service. I didn't have the money but because I didn't want to go through the court journey again, I borrowed the money from my mom and aunt. I sent him the money. Only to find out later that he was out with a girl who was about to be a permanent feature in my story. They even used my Airbnb credit that I was saving to use with the kids. On top of that I funded their day with the money I borrowed from my mom and aunt. When I said in the beginning this guy was the devil himself, I was not joking. A week later my car supposedly broke down, but he didn't want me to claim from insurance he said he will fix it. He started coming home with a new Renault Cleo. From the get-go you could just see that this was a woman's car but again he said it was a friend's car. This was during COVID the first hard lock and he was driving around in this time without getting arrested because he had a smooth tongue and ways of getting out of trouble. The car would be locked down in our house when I would ask him what is the owner using when their car is locked down with us, he would say they have many cars. The car became part of the family he would even take the kids to school with it. Doctors' visits with my son would be taken in this car even when my car was back from the "repairs". He would take pictures of both cars in the garage and post them everywhere saying it was his cars.

The first day the car slept in my garage I had a very strange dream that when I woke up from the dream, I asked him if he was cheating on me of which he denied. This recurring dream

## Relationships with strings attached

would happen and intensify every time this car would be in my garage. One day I dreamt I was even in the woman's house, and it tuned out I literally went to the woman's house in my dream hahahahaha. That was the strangest period of my life. He would deny all my dreams every time even called me a family sangoma whenever I would tell him my dream and the fact that I now know the owner of the car and where she lived. He still would deny but now I had a little relief because the woman was now the one depositing into the salary account. I would deposit small amounts occasionally. 4 months into the new place we had to move out because he was not paying rent on time, so he found us a cheaper place that he paid for with the other woman's money in the first month.

*Remember I am telling you what I know now or what I later found out, at the time he told me he got the money from one of his business partners. He was supposed to return it after a month but in that month, he was in hiding never used his phone, got a small burner phone and he told this "partner" that he was in jail because he did not follow through with some of his community work. Remember this month for later in the chapter!*

When we moved to the other house the neighbour had an old BMW that was sitting in his yard with flat tires that you could see it was sitting there for more than 10 years. He managed to convince the girl to give him R100 000 to buy it. They were literally dating for only a month, and she gave him that money. Of course, I found out about this a year later but that was the type of person I let in my house and let him be close to my kids. I even gave him a child. When we moved to the other house, I guess we only moved there alone because he only stayed with us for one month (this was the month that he was in hiding, remember he told his "partner" that he was in jail but it turned out the partner was a new girlfriend) after that he would do rotational visits during my pay day, stay one week ensure he gets the money he needs to go to another rotational home. He would say he is doing business deals, and these deals would require him to have money in his bank account. One day I found very expensive shoes and clothes he was hiding in a cooler box in the garage. He bought these things with my money that he said was for a business deal. He would now take loans because "his" credit profile was good. He used the loans to buy himself things and take out other girls. He was so deep into his lies that he brought in more girls. He would also occasionally drive the Yaris if he was not driving his regular Cleo.

Before his official move out, he drove the Cleo to come to our son's first birthday, on his way back to his woman he bumped the car. This was after I told him I was uneasy about this car parked in my garage every time it's here it's like I time travel in my dream into another woman's life. This bothered me until I asked my cousin to check the license plates only to confirm what I already knew, now I just knew I was not going crazy. He came apologising saying he should have listened to me now he is in trouble after bumping this woman's car. In the middle of the night the woman called him he went rushing there. The next morning, he was posting pictures of how the woman bought him expensive perfume because she was sad, he had an accident. I guess it was to spite me because I never did that when he was in an accident with my car, knowing that he never forgets things.

The following month was my bonus month. He started devising a plan of how to get this money from me. Funny enough I knew when he all of a sudden started confessing about the things he was doing and saying the woman I found out about who owns the car is a prostitute they use as part of their business, she was bait to get the rich men to fall for their business. I knew all he was saying was lies, but I still let him stay in my house. Maybe he was putting something in my food hence he was always insisting on cooking in-fact I would see him carrying traditional herbs but never thought they could work on me. At this point my mom was telling me every day that she is worried about my safety saying she was uneasy about this guy I need to let him out my house otherwise he will kill me. I couldn't believe why my mom would think he would kill me. I knew he was not a good person but not to the point of killing me. Come

## Relationships with strings attached

bonus time he devised a story of me deposing R44 000 into "his" account and that he will return it back to my account on the same day because his business partners want to use his account to pitch for a deal and there must be money in the account. He wanted more but I lied and said I will be left with R44 000 after paying bills and he still did not think to ask for R20 000 at least he wanted all of it. On pay day I was a nervous wreck because I knew he was lying but I did not have a plan. I phoned my other cousin back home we devised a plan but still could not follow through with it. I went to mug and bean very early in the morning. At this time, I had no car I was using bolt/uber because he had sent my car to get fixed by the "bush mechanics" in Olievenhoutbosch. I ordered breakfast talked to my mom told her I will be sending her money part of me wanted to send her all my money, but I was afraid of what was waiting for me back home if I don't send him this money. At this stage I started thinking about mom's words. He was calling me none stop asking me when am I sending the money because his business partners are waiting. I went home found him all dressed up like he was going to a wedding. He asked me about the money I asked him when will he return it because I have to pay my son's school fees and give my mom money. He got angry and reminded me that we had already spoken about this. I deposited the money; it did not take him even 5 minutes to walk to where he was parking the Cleo since I told him I don't want it in my garage anymore. His words were, I must not worry about the car he is using the girl since she is just a prostitute, they are using to get rich white men to do business with them, but he would respect my wishes and ask for parking by the neighbour's house.

The whole day I was wallowing in regret and anxiety that was the worst birthday month in my whole entire life. I told my cousin what I did, and he was so disappointed he even said he would not tell my mom because she would be so disappointed in my decision. How could I give away my kid's money like that? I waited for him to come back home so that he can give me the money. He came back home in the afternoon and started

## Relationships with strings attached

cooking. He didn't even see that I had bought the kids take away but did not eat because I had no appetite. I was stressed even vomiting from the stress and anxiety. He came to my room to tell me he has cooked we must all come eat together he will tell me about the business deal. I asked him when he will deposit the money. He got so angry that he threw his phone on the wall. After doing this stunt he now blamed me for making him angry meaning he now cannot transfer the money because his phone is broken. I nearly had a heart attack from anger, he left the house without eating because he said he was going to Sunnyside to try and find people to fix the phone. He came back home 3 hours later telling me he left the phone but could deposit some money to another account because he now needed money to pay for the phone and he wanted to give me some money to give my mom. They charged him R5000 to fix the phone. Meaning I was now going to get back R39 000. I said its fine just give me back my money. Then he asked me how much I wanted to give my mom I said I can't tell you that just give me my money he said he will give me after he gets his phone. He left and came back again carrying a pink suitcase. When I say pink, I mean bright pink. He packed all his things and told me that he can't be with me anymore because I don't trust him. How convenient after I had just given him my money. He left and the next morning he only deposited R3 000 saying he will deposit the rest later of which he never did.

He would come occasionally on the woman's pay days bringing groceries. At this point I was content with him gone and when he came, I would not even be angry I would take the groceries and watch him leave. My mom would even be angry that I took the groceries. Every time he would tell me a story of how he will pay me back, even went to my son's school to buy some more time for the school fees I should not worry. The school did tell me that he came to make arrangement hence they never chased my son out of school but all that going to school was in vain in the long run. He disappeared from our lives for 4 months at this time he was staying in a flat that he told me he

## Relationships with strings attached

was applying for it for his friend only to find he was planning to stay with his girlfriend there and the girl did not agree because her family would not allow her to vat n sat. His plan was to use my money to pay for few months and later let the girl pay rent did not work. He was now making fraudulent papers to work as proof of payment, and he got deeper into trouble as he would call me to try and bail him out using the lawyer my friend referred. One time his girlfriend called police on him because apparently now he was owning a gun. He called to apologize to me for ill-treating me and told me all that was happening in his life. At this time, I had now moved to a more affordable place closer to the Gautrain station. I was no longer feeling the burden of having someone around draining my finances. For the first time in a long time, I was happy again and was having money to save again at the end of the month. My son was failed by the school because of not paying school fees. I had to make a plan to put him in an online school so that he does not repeat a grade because of my dumbness. He did not struggle in the school in fact he excelled even more than before. I was so happy that I did not ruin his life.

One day I dreamt that my car was being striped. I called him and told him about this dream, and he took me to the car to show me that it was still being fixed. I couldn't believe why it was taking so long to fix it. But at this time, I was at peace that he was no longer my problem. I had the same dream about the car again so now because I knew where the car was, I decided to go with an uber to go check it out alone. I found them working on the car. I asked them when will they finish and what was wrong with the car. The guys were shocked as to why I was asking them this. I told them that that was my car, and I was still paying the bank instalment for it. They were shocked because guy had sold it to another guy and the new car owner was now putting in extras. The car was fixed a long time ago it came at the same time with the Cleo, and he used some of the money he got from selling my car to pay for the damages from the Cleo. If I didn't faint that day I never will, I found out through all the series of shocking news that I am actually very strong. The person that bought the car came to the place surprisingly just when I was talking to the people. I had asked the uber guy to wait for me because I just wanted to find out how far are the repairs for my car. He was so shocked when I told him that I just found out that my car was sold while I am still paying instalment. Sold by someone I have a child with.

I phoned him still in shock and he was so angry at me something that did not bother me anymore. He told me that now I have ruined his plan because he was still trying to organize money to buy back the car before I could even find out. The other car that he had bought from our neighbours' yard was also being fixed there, fixed by the money that was from selling my car. He started saying now they are going to take his car. He did not care that he sold my car now he was blaming me for mingling in things that don't concern me. Imagine if I ignored my dream, I would not have found out that my car was sold without my knowledge.

During this time my mom passed away and reflexes I guess he was the only person I could think of when I got the news. He came to my house within minutes, and I got the news at almost midnight. He apparently ran from his place to mine and because it was still during COVID, police stopped him and luckily gave him a lift that's how he got to me so quick because now he did not drive the Cleo regularly, remember the girl got him arrested. He offered to take us home I was still confused as to how I will get home remember my car was sold. He disappeared the whole day trying to organize a car to get us home. I used this time to claim from my funeral cover and my other cousin from Centurion the one that was telling me that the guy is not good for me in the beginning was helping me out with the driving up and down even advised me to hire a car and not wait for this guy to take me home. He still didn't want him around me especially since he also saw him in the girl's house when he went to a party in the same area that the girl stayed. He told me that the wife's friend told them the guy practically lived there and he couldn't

## Relationships with strings attached

tell me another miner detail that he saw that I saw for myself in a dream later on in the year. I didn't trust if I was going to be able to drive all the way with just the kids for such a long distance especially knowing I am driving home to my mom's funeral whom I could not visit for the first December ever because I did not have a car and did not want kids in public transport during the pandemic.

He called later in the evening to tell me he managed to get a car, but we will have to go very early in the morning because he told the owner of the car that he is going for an interview. I wanted to see which car he was coming with. In the morning, he can with the Cleo. I was like you know what let me just go bury my mom. He drove us home immediately when we got to Ladysmith the girl started calling none stop I guess her car tracker started notifying her that the car was no longer in Gauteng. Can you imagine having to deal with the loss of your pillar while being driven home by your X who is your baby daddy in his current girlfriends' car whom he met while living in your house, driving your car flexing with a fake salary that was your money. Yah I really don't know how I survived this phase of my life.

Everyone was shocked that I am being dropped by him, but we quickly got consumed by the reason I was home. He came to get us a week later after the funeral again in the Cleo. My cousin who was the one helping me to get the owner of the license plate saw the car and was like my sister really are you bewitched or what. But I just walked away in shame and got in the car with my kids, and we drove back to Gauteng. When we got home, we found he pulled the same stunt he pulled when we first met. He brought all his things to my new place. This time he got access to my place via my helper because I had not given him any of my keys. I couldn't believe this and had no power to fight literally I just watched the movie play out. Guy was now in hiding remember he was no longer paying rent using fake proof of payments so apparently the rental agent was looking for him. His Yaris girl was looking for him as well because apparently, he sold her car too. The girl kept calling me telling me she knows I am with him she knows where my kids go to school she will find me.

There I was now being threatened for something I knew nothing about. For two months he would play this game of coming to my house and going to Cleo house at this point I was watching a movie waiting for it to finish for good. I think guy was thinking I am going to get money from my mom's death he would ask me for money, and I would deny him. But one time he did trick me to giving him R4000 I don't even know how I gave him after all the drama, but I gave him. This era of my life was the most confusing and most draining because I had all the evidence to have this guy locked up, I stayed in an area where I could easily chase him out and tell the security guard not to let him in but I was powerless and actionless, I was not even in love with the guy instead I wanted nothing to do with him yet here I was living with him.

Two months later I got a promotion that needed me to move to KZN I think this was just my mom doing her magic in heaven to get me away from this guy because there was no shaking him away from me. When I moved, he wanted to move with me saying he wants to start a new leaf in life. One day I had a dream his girl was giving birth, and her family came to my house to announce that she is pregnant with his child, and she is on her way to hospital to give birth and he was with her. They were apologising for all the wrong that has been done to me even saying they thought this guy was good for their daughter and they now want nothing to do with him. I woke up from the dream and called him as usual he denied the pregnancy. I then moved to KZN I started by staying with my sister. All my kids were home schooled, and it was less stress when I was at work, they were all home with a helper or my sister sometimes. One day I had a dream my mom telling me to stay away from this guy and I was about to move to my own place, and he was planning to move in with us.

Relationships with strings attached

At this point I was now heavily praying for God to remove him from my life and cancel whatever spell he had on me. The next morning when I got to work, Ms Cleo called me with a private number. When she told me her name, I knew who I was talking too. She was calling to let me know that she has a 2-month-old baby with the guy and that she has been stalking my Facebook page trying to make sense of everything. Guy told her we were long broken up when they met but she was surprised my child was less than a year when they met, and he saw me posting pictures with him. She eventually realized the places he was going to with her car was my place. She apparently got pregnant the first time they slept together that time when he was frequenting Midrand selling avocados. She said she was shocked that her twin sister's avocado delivery was being delivered by a handsome guy driving a nice BMW. She started ordering avocados even though she never ate them. Eventually they went out (remember that night he got arrested with Nigerians) and on that very night slept together and she got pregnant. That's when he started using her car, she would get lifts from her twin sister to go around as the guy felt entitled to her car from the get go. She confirmed a lot of things even my dreams of 2 girls coming into my house and demanding wine, was me dreaming about twins etc.

As she was narrating her relationship troubles, I couldn't understand how this guy managed to manipulate women so easily. I suddenly started thinking the reason he loved cooking so much was perhaps where he administered his "juju" on us because I really was under a spell. This girl was working in the legal department of a financial institution an admitted attorney, yet she was scared for her life, financially drained just like me now having to raise his child alone. There was a time I saw him carrying muthi/juju "traditional herbs" and he told me someone gave him to help him with his "business deals" and the business deals he was actually, talking about were not deals because I eventually found out from her phone call that all the documents, he was showing me and laptop screenshots were actually this girl's work information, there were no business deals at all. I somehow knew this, did nothing and the phone call was just confirmation that I was not dreaming these things or starting to lose my mind.

The Yaris owner was also a professional she even had older kids as she was much older than us. I guess her old age helped her from getting a child. This lady also knew about the Yaris lady and knew the story of her car being sold as she was there when the car was sold. She also mentioned that he disappeared for a month after he had borrowed R12000 from her on the first few days that they met (remember the 1 months' rent he got from a business partner). When he reappeared it was when she found out she was pregnant and that was when he convinced her to borrow him more money to buy that old car from my new neighbour. When she ended the phone call, she said she was scared for her life as the guy was aggressive and physically abusive with her. She had tried everything to get rid of him, but he kept coming back to her and manipulating security guards to get access to her house. But just like me she never tried to get him arrested although she once reported him for having a gun pointed at her, she later dropped the charges.

This relationship finally reached a dead stop after the pregnancy reveal, in the few months that he tried to come back in my life I was already feeling the financial pinch. I went through a 21-day prayer and fasting just to cut myself from him. He came to my house in KZN but couldn't stay long it was as if something was burning him. After my fasting I suddenly got the edge to pack away all his things that he had left in my house and sent them to him with an Intercape bus.

That was the last I heard from him. I have been freed from him ever since. I truly then believed he was from the devil because it took prayer and fasting to get rid of him. Nothing worked even my mom's warning. I mean everyone was warning me about him even my soul was tired of him, but it took prayer and fasting to get him out of my life. The fact that what I wrote about this experience is so long yet not everything I went through at the hands of this demon that was using him to torment my life it's just crazy. I am just happy that God rescued me out of these chains with the peace that surpasses all understanding. I really experienced the love of God through Christ Jesus in this relationship. I also think even though our encounter was very bad I really grew spiritually through this experience, it was with him that my dream life started really showing me that God speaks. It was happening before but with him my dreams were more accurate and frequent it was just on another level.

This chapter of my life was very long and draining, physically, emotionally even financially. I look back and wonder sometimes where I would be in life had I not gone on that breakfast date. But I guess we take the positive and learn from the negative.

# REFLECTION

I wouldn't be doing any justice to myself and this process of healing through writing my journey if I don't write about my lost journey. Well in between the time I left my over 10-year relationship with Angela and Tiro's dad. The man I thought would be my husband my forever. I remember we were engaged on and off for over 4 years. By on and off I mean there was one time he took my ring saying his uncles wanted to see it. I didn't see anything wrong with that in fact what were we doing with western traditions of engagements. I thought him showing his uncle's my ring was to start the talks of going to my parents for lobola negotiations (naïve me thought so I guess).

On the other hand, I had to go to work and face colleagues asking me what happened to my ring. The answer was always "we were young and thinking ahead of our traditions we just want to do things right with the elders involved. Of course that was me saving face, he never gave me any explanation as to why he was taking off my ring to go and show his uncles. While I was on the wait, he started dating a sangoma (traditional healer) girl. I found out about this relationship without even looking just like all other relationships he would try to have on the side. I can't even explain it, but it was like as soon as he starts something some drama would happen for me to find out what was going on. This time around my sister was visiting and he found it ok to go missing with my car for the whole weekend. He would call to say he was on the way but would not make it home. I started

## Relationships with strings attached

shouting at him telling him that he was embarrassing me while my sister was visiting now it looked like it was a norm, and he had never done that before. When he eventually came back, he could not sleep that night, he woke up in the middle of the night to tell me that my sister has bad spirits. He found this out from a friend that was a sangoma (whom I later found out that they were dating).

He packed his things and went to his parent's house in Pretoria West. I was so upset with him accusing my sister like that especially because my sister had been nothing but kind to him even when he went missing with my car, she said nothing. My sister had helped us countless times and she was known to be our go to person for prayer and the word of God now she was bringing bad spirits? I was happy he moved out, but we were still together until I broke up with him after I found him with the sangoma when his car broke down after getting Angela from creche. If he could fetch our daughter from creche with another woman, I knew there must not be a future for us. I mean there was no respect anymore. The brake up was short lived (3 months to be exact) because he came back with the ring and an apology, that is when I got pregnant with Tiro but that was short lived, he was no longer the same. I started even being scared for my life around him. When Tiro was a few months old I gave him back his ring because I was tired of being called Mrs. Molefe especially as I could see there was no plans of moving forward, the ring was just to stop me while he was still freely on the lookout.

It took me three years to get over this relationship. Although I didn't do any healing work, I tried therapy for one day. I realised it wasn't for me. Because I didn't do any healing work, I was literally a walking wounded soul vulnerable to any and everything that came my way. I was going to church, but it was not enough healing, it was more of a routine than really walking with God. On one side I was also feeling stuck in my career. This state I was in was the perfect door for the devil to walk in. Suddenly, my friend referred me to a white medium that everyone in her workplace was going to. She convinced me to go see her as she was also going because we both needed answers to our stagnant life. I never believed in such however I was curious.

Suddenly everything about spiritual healing started popping up on my timeline. I even began to follow a lady that I was introduced to who was a money coach, but all her conversations shifted more and more into this believing in the universe teachings. I was then more open to even consider taking up my friends advise to go see a medium. I went there for my career, but she started telling me about my relationships and why they fail. This was then an open portal for destruction in my life. I started looking for this guy she mentioned would be my husband. I started attracting other mediums, sangomas, healers, etc. it was just out of hand. I kept going back to this medium because somehow it felt good hearing about my future and talking to my dad and later my mom who were both no longer with me.

But looking back the more I went there the more I attracted bad experiences. I made bad relationship choices because I was looking for this man, she always told me was looking for me, however, I was so blinded to even see that with every consultation the description of this person would change. At some point I went with her with my X from the previous chapter and she told us the ancestors were happy for us to meet and be married which was a recipe for disaster because I think I stayed longer in that toxic relationship because of what was said in that consultation with the medium. I was so far from God, yet I was still going to Church.

It took me over 4 years to realize I was playing with God's purpose for my life. My life was going from bad to worse each and every year and each year I was learning new things that were taking me further and further away from God. It took me being in the lowest point when I was now raising 3 kids alone in a house, I would not even pick for myself in my lowest of lowest

## Relationships with strings attached

day. But I had allowed a man to turn my life upside down so much that he left me with a small child and 2 not so big kids to raise alone in a very bad area. I sank into so much depression that only God took me out. I remember when I decided to move out the house that my X got for us after he stopped paying rent in that nice golf estate I loved so much. I went to the property24 website, and the house was just listed for a few minutes. Something said contact the owner. After talking to her she removed the listing, and we met to view the house but before viewing the house we sat in her car and had a long chat. She didn't know that on that day she re introduced me to God not by reading the bible but by being able to listen to my story, gave me Godly advice and allowed me a chance to stay in her late sister's house without even doing background checks. She had a horrible tenant experience before me and was so excited to give this place to me and the kids. Living in that house was so peaceful and marked the turning point of my life because it was there where I really started having a relationship with God. I stayed there for 6 months before moving to KZN, but it was a place that truly started my healing journey.

While reflecting on everything I went through I realised that from a young age I was already walking under set demonic traps that later in life showed themselves as relationship problems, but it was beyond that. I was being set up for failure in every area of my life i.e. my finances, my properties (I literally lost properties that I bought at a young age), my car got stolen in one relationship, got sold in another relationship, I was without a car for years whereas I was in a well-paying job. When I got to buy the car that I always wanted, I couldn't keep it because I was being scammed by the mechanic that was supposed to just service it but always brought problems that made the car not a pleasure to have. I know all these sound like material things, but they were serious distractions because I couldn't focus on God. I had to move from house to house, had to deal with ensuring my kids get to school, get food, get to have a life that won't show that I am raising them alone.

## Relationships with strings attached

There was no peace in my life year after year, but all of this was because of demonic attacks that were hiding as the different strings that seemed to come through relationships. I started writing this book thinking I had to cut the strings that were attached in my life through relationships but I had to find my Journey back to God and do what he had purposed me to do and that had to start with me getting deliverance from all the demonic forces that got an open door in my life before I was even born through generational curses and started manifesting when I was only 5 years old.

Without going deep into scripture, that will be in my next book. I just want to leave you with this verse to help you understand that even though things may happen, living you helpless or hopeless there is hope in Jesus Christ who came to save us and give us everlasting love. I may not have all the answers or have completely healed but this verse always gives me perspective on how much God is on my side and has fought over all that tried to keep my soul captive.

*"Having cancelled the charge of our legal indebtedness, which stood against us and condemned us; he has taken it away, nailing it to the cross. And having disarmed the powers and authorities, he made a public spectacle of them, triumphing over them by the cross."* Colossians 2: 14 & 15 NIV

# CHAPTER 8

# I THOUGHT I WAS HEALED

I thought I was healed but there was another so-called King that was still coming to give me the final destruction. I believe this relationship came to either add the last string or to give me the scissors to finally cut all the strings off my life and find a good and healthy relationship. There was a time I was so angry with him that I said this to him "You call yourself a King but you're in actual fact a servant, a servant for ASS" hahaha I was really angry. Here is a brief reflection of this time in my life and why I was so angry.

This will not be a long chapter, but I felt it was also necessary to include because it may help someone understand that healing is really not a destination but a journey. When I met this guy, I thought I was healed I thought nothing can ever be as bad as what I went through. Besides now I was armed with the armour of God. I thought I knew what I was getting myself into and I was not going to fall for anything that was planning to break me. Boy, was I wrong or was I completely wrong hahahahaha. I was still an infant in this healing journey, and I guess this relationship was needed to show me another side of me that needed serious healing. Ok here is a brief overview it was a lot, but I really don't think he deserved a chapter but anyways here goes. It was almost a year that I had finally cut myself off demon possessed guy hahahaha. I know that's extreme but let's go with the name. I was back to my happy space, even though my credit was messed up because I had to stop paying for my car in order for the bank to repossess it (remember the car story from the previous chapter). I never opened a case against X when he sold my car my because well my excuse was that the court visits really tormented me in this relationship, and I was not about to go through that agian. Anyway, the bank gave me a great deal after they repossessed my car. I had to pay a small amount for them to remove the blacklist however my credit was already damaged. For some strange reason this did not bother me. I was happy content and living my best life with the kids. I couldn't get any credit, but I was happy. The pension money from my resignation also took its time to come out. It took over a year for me to get my money but I guess it was deliberate because if it came out early the guy would have finished it because he already had plans with my money in fact he had told his girlfriend that he got a nice contract in KZN which will pay him a nice lump sum after 3 months, that lump sum was my pension, can you imagine hahahahaha.

With God's divine protection the lump sum delayed for over a year. In this time, I started taking care of myself, getting closer to God and doing banting diet plus home exercises. I lost more than 20 kg's I was happy and in the best head space I was ever in for the longest of time. One day I decided to go to the pharmacy to buy vitamin supplements to support my weight loss journey. I was following this other Keto doctor on YouTube who was stressing the importance of drinking these vitamins while you're on the weight loss journey. While I was looking for these pills this guy started shouting "makoti (wife). I ignored it, again he shouted makoti then I looked back and said are you talking to me he said yes, I am talking to you. I was like no I am not married he laughed and said you are my family's makoti. We laughed and I told him, that could never be he looked so young he could have been same age as my niece. But he lied about his age, and we started shopping together as if we came to the shop together. He was working there so it was as if he was helping me to shop. When I was done shopping, he asked for my phone, and I gave him. He asked me to put the password because he was fascinated by the camera he wanted to see more features. I did that and he put his name and number on the contact list and sent himself a WhatsApp. This was the beginning of him sending me messages calling me makoti.

I googled him and found out he had recently done an interview on the local news and his age was way less than what he told me but at this stage I was enjoying the attention and distraction. Fast-forward we started dating. I would occasionally visit him, and his place was not the best, but I was still not firm enough to choose what was best for me. I went with the flow. He was good looking and good company. I convinced myself that I am not looking for marriage so it couldn't hurt being with him. We started going out often, he loved to eat so we would restaurant hop a lot even driving to Durban just to try out a restaurant. It was fun I am not going to lie. When I moved to a new place, he helped me move. (I moved a lot since the time I sold my house back in Centurion.). A week in he was evicted from his place because he was not paying rent, so I offered the outside room for him to use while he was getting his feet off the ground as he was fired/resigned from the pharmacy and started working at some gym. In my head I was helping a boyfriend, and he was not going to be staying with me but staying in the outbuilding. Who was I kidding the outbuilding ended up being the storeroom for his things, but he was always in my house.

We became so close, and everything was nice, but I started seeing how he was too much of a flirt and he literally called all the girls on his social media makoti in their comments. I had access to his social media accounts as I was helping him grow his audience and I would see how much he was in so many girls DM's asking them out. Some it was the other way around, as the girls were asking him out. I would pretend like it was not bothering me. Anyways I already thought I have been through the worst this is nothing he is just being a man trying to be famous. He never wanted to be intimate that much, I was fine with it as sex is really not everything or so I thought hahahaha.

## Relationships with strings attached

We started now making plans together even went on an international trip to Dubai. He was going to a body building competition and it was my 40th birthday so it was a perfect celebration we shared the funding for the trip although I contributed more. I didn't mind as this was my first international trip. I was very happy. But before the trip my helper had overhead him talking to a girl over the phone and she was not happy and told me about the whole conversation. I confronted him about it, and he reminded me that we were not married and that him being in my house was temporary I must remember I offered to help him when he was evicted, he is grateful, but I must not think we are married. Now my brain went into past trauma mode I shut down and went to living on auto pilot. Tickets were booked already I could still cancel the trip, but I was looking forward to going to Dubai. Time for Dubai came we were happy, but it was not the same. We were not even intimate anymore but in a relationship. He would make excuses that it was the supplements and the stress of the competition, but I would see messages of him asking for sex from girls he would meet for the first time at the gym. It's like he had this thrill of having sex with a new girl every single day.

We tried or I tried to enjoy myself in Dubai I was not about to let my money go to waste. It was good minus the intimacy it was literary as if I went there with a friend. He did not win which gave him an excuse to not be in a good mood for the majority of the stay there, but he made sure he would take my card to go to the gym to get connections for work. He would go with a taxi twice a day. The taxi ride was R600 a trip meaning it was R1200 a day just to go to the gym and he would get there and buy himself expensive gym wear. One day I decided to move money from that account to another and I switched off my phone. He nearly got arrested that day, but he couldn't go to the gym because he didn't have money. At this point I was really fed up with him. I went out and had the best last night in Dubai while he was stuck in the room trying to get me and my phones were off. I later found out on that day he was meeting with another girl he even took one of my jackets that had his brand to give to the girl, but the meet up never happened, and we were leaving the next day so he left the jacket with our reception for the girl to come collect. I remember seeing he posted her wearing my jacket on his brands page.

Anyways this relationship was slowly dying, and I was not about to drain myself like I did before. The happy moments were becoming less and less. The breaking point was the December holidays that he said we would use to re kindle our relationship, but it was the time he showed me real flames. In January he started posting me a lot on his WhatsApp which was strange. So, on this one time he did that I took his phone while he was asleep and reposted myself with the same captions "makoti" etc. and I took his phone with on my way to Durban with the kids. The messages that came from so many girls after that was crazy. Young, old, black Indian etc. All complaining about how he used them for one-night stands. One was even threatening to kill me because he had been asking him about me, but he would lie all the time. This one they were together for almost a year now on and off.

He was so angry with me I guess people started calling him from his other phone. I found him furious, and he had broken my door and bed. That was when my senses came to life, and I chased him out of my house. He moved to the outside room and would bring girls over. It was the first time in my life I had ever met a guy that had so many girlfriends and 1 night stands I would even feel sorry for him. It took 3 months and a protection order to get him out of my yard.

Well, I guess after this drama ended and my dreams again taking me out of this situation. I realised that I thought I was healed but I was nowhere near healing. It was at this stage that I took a decision to fully commit to God and forget about life things that take me away from him especially sex before marriage. I decided to be celibate and if I don't meet my husband I decided to remain this way till death. I am not sure what the

## Relationships with strings attached

future holds for me but one thing I know for sure relationships showed me flames but I am grateful for the lessons and getting out alive and sane every time.

# CHAPTER 9

# AN UNFAILING LOVE

I recall the days when the burden of the world felt unbearable. My mind was stuck in zombie mode as what my friend and I would call it. Each morning, getting out of bed was an effort. My body was numb, my spirit lost. It felt like an endless cold winter had found a spot in my soul, with no spring in sight. Friends and family were there, work was keeping me busy but that was not enough. I couldn't shake the feeling that even God had turned His back on me. Opening the bible or even reading a bible verse as it came up on my Facebook feed was a brain attack. Depression is a crafty thief indeed, where there was once unmatched joy in my life it was replaced with hopelessness. I didn't know I was depressed until my mom would call me every day to force me to get out of bed. Going to work was a burden but at least when I was around my colleagues I would escape reality a bit. My prayers felt like words with no meaning. I started questioning everything, especially my faith. It seemed as though God had forgotten me, or worse, was deliberately silent. This was a betrayal that cut the deepest. I had always believed in a God and having angels assigned to protect me. Now, I felt abandoned, lost in an ocean of despair with no horizon in sight. I was constantly looking for answers outside what I was taught or believed in. Having faith in the unknown seemed to be a futile exercise. Suddenly what I had read in an article about the enemy using your character flaw as a legal right against God's plans for you was my reality. The character flaws being anger, bitterness, resentment, unforgiveness, offence and pride were all finding a space in my daily life. Little did I know that this was the enemy's way (the devil) to keep me stuck in what looked like depression, but it was really his plan to derail my purpose here on earth and to steal whatever peace that was still promised in my current life and future. In this period, I began grabbing for anything that promised relief. Depression has a way of making a small issue big and moving you from calm to panic mode. As mentioned in previous chapters friends, well-meaning and concerned, suggested alternatives. They spoke of mediums, tarot card readers, and spiritual healers as if they would magically make everything feel better. "What do you have to lose?" they would say. And really at that state I felt like I had nothing more to lose than what I had been through.

My first encounter with a medium was something I could never imagine. In fact, the night before I felt so much paranoia it was as if there was someone following me and looking at me through a glass frame or mirror. She was very friendly and greeted me with a beautiful smile as I walked in her consulting room that looked nothing like what I had imagined. It looked more like I was consulting a medical doctor. Her first words were "Your grandmother is already with you; can I call your father as well he is sitting outside?" I was shocked but relieved at the same time that finally I will get answers. She told me things that no one else could have known, intimate details that only I knew about. For a moment, it was comforting to think there might be a connection to something greater, something beyond my comprehension. I already had that connection with God through Jesus, but the enemy was so bent on making me feel like what I knew was nothing and what I was getting exposed to was the ultimate solution I had been looking for. Suddenly, I started getting suggestion of tarot card readers on my e-mail, social media feeds etc. it was as if I was now attracting this world, I knew existed but was never interested in.

## Relationships with strings attached

I was now deep in despair right in the middle of the enemy's camp. All these things promised solutions but just like a bad dream I was just moving from 1 maze to another with no real solution in sight. Then there were the spiritual healers, sangomas etc, each with their unique approach to mending my fractured soul. Some used crystals, others energy work, and a few combined various rituals meant to cleanse and restore. They spoke of the chakras, auras, and energies that emanated from the universe and within me. I would find myself attending live session to align my chakras; to open my third eye hey it was just a lot. These sessions did not even leave me with a sense of brief peace, it was all just broken pieces in a faded glass like the song would say. Thinking of that time of my life scares me even as I write in past tense. I know it seems like I keep on writing about the same thing when it comes to this time, but I think God really wants me to emphasis this part of my journey. As I started re-reading the bible I kept realising the many times God mentioned how much he despises us believing or worshiping idols or false God's. I believe the enemy sent me down this path mirroring my hurt with despair and luring me to a world that was to take me further away from the presence and love of God. The more I invested more time, money, and hope into these practices' things were just falling apart. I would be setting my intentions with the moon cycles and find myself making bad financial decisions that would set me 10 steps back. The realisation that not everything that I had labelled as hurt was really hurt, it was actually a lesson for me to get to the next level, came to me when I was now exhausted by everything. I realised or woke up from the trans that was making sure I held on to all the hurt, but this was not helping me instead it was a stumbling block to my healing. But all was not lost as we serve a God that is always waiting for you to get to the aha moment. He couldn't wait to say welcome my child I have been waiting for you with open arms. It didn't matter how many times I fell He still called me HIS and this is how I found my way back home just like the prodigal son. The turning point was not from a sangoma or a card reading, but from within. In the quiet moments of introspection, I began to see that the power I sought outside was already within me. It wasn't about what the mediums, the cards, or the healers said. It was about reclaiming my strength, my faith, and my connection to God on my own terms. Slowly, I started trusting what was already there deep inside me. I turned inward, seeking solace in praise, worship, meditating on the word of God and prayer, not as a plea for rescue but as a way to reconnect with myself and my faith. I began to see that God hadn't abandoned me. I had simply lost sight of Him in my search for external answers, in my search for a life partner, in my search for peace. The journey back was not easy, but it was mine to take. The relationships with strings attached throughout the book taught me a lot about vulnerability and the human need for connection and understanding. But they also showed me that true healing begins with self-love and faith in God.

I emerged from the depths of my despair, not unscathed, but stronger, more resilient, and more attuned to the whispers of my soul and the silent presence of the divine. Armed with the word of God as my scissor. I might have not reached or may reach my "complete healing" however as I navigate life, I had to understand that "Healing is a journey and not a destination". I find peace knowing that I don't have to walk this journey alone I have God by my side always.

May you find the same peace.

# CHAPTER 10

# FINDING MY WAY OUT OF - THE DEPTHS OF DESPAIR

Relationships sometimes promise balance, peace and stability, what happens when all of this is not in place? This may not necessarily be found in a relationship with another person, but a connection to something extremely greater, more eternal. It is here, where, I found the extent of God's love, a love that has remained steady even when human connections failed.

Throughout the ups and downs of my journey I often found myself feeling aimless/ lost. Each relationship, no matter how promising in the beginning, eventually led me to a place of disappointment and hurt. As I navigated the end of these relationships, I often wondered if there was a love that could truly withstand the tests of time and the flaws of human nature. I questioned whether such a love existed beyond the stories told in fairy tales and songs.

The concept of God's love wasn't new to me; it had been a part of my life from childhood. But it wasn't until I found myself at the lowest points of my romantic failures that I began to understand its significance. When I was in the midst of another heartbreak, and my heart ached with the familiar pain of abandonment, it was then that I began to feel the quiet whisper of God's unwavering presence. Unlike the momentary

## Relationships with strings attached

assurances of human love, God's love felt different steady and all-complete. It was there during sleepless nights with tears and unanswered questions. It was there when I felt completely alone, rejected by the ones I had given my love to. In those moments, I observed a gentle, reassuring presence, a love that didn't require anything in return but simply existed, waiting for me to notice it.

I can observe how God's love was a part of my journey, even when I didn't recognize it. It was in the supportive friends who stood by me, in the family members who held me close when I was breaking apart, and in the quiet moments of solitude where I found unexpected peace.

God's love was in the fates, the small miracles that brought me forward when I was ready to give up. It was in the strangers' smiles and the kindness of those who saw my pain and offered a hand. There were times I felt undeserving of such love, especially when my mistakes in relationships were so obvious. The guilt and shame that followed these failed relationships often clouded my view, convincing me that I was too flawed to be worthy of any love, let alone one as pure as God's love. Yet, in those moments, I began to understand a deeper truth: God's love is not about worthiness. It is about grace. It is unconditional and unearned, given freely and abundantly, irrespective of my failures. As I began to embrace this divine love, I found a new sense of wholeness. It did not erase the pain of my failed relationships, but it gave me the strength to move beyond them. God's love became a lens through which I could see my own value, not based on the validation of another person, but on the worth given to me by God. It was a love that lifted me from the shame of my brokenness and taught me to love myself again. In this journey, I also learned to forgive not only those who had hurt me but also myself.

Forgiveness became a central part of my healing, allowing me to let go of the burdens I had carried for so long. With every relationship that ended, I had collected pieces of bitterness and regret. God's love helped me to release these fragments, replacing them with compassion and understanding. As I continue to navigate the complexities of love and relationships, I hold on to the truth that there is a love that will never fail me. It is a love that transcends the limitations of human affection, a love that is steadfast and unwavering. This love is my anchor, grounding me when the storms of life threaten to overwhelm. It is a love that sees me as I am, with all my imperfections, and embraces me fully. As I look forward, I do so with the assurance that this love will continue to guide me, healing my wounds and filling my heart with hope.

God's love is my reminder that even in the face of broken human connections, there is a love that remains unbroken a love that is perfect, eternal, and always enough.

May you also find this love

# BONUS CHAPTER

# THE FOREIGN LOVE

Have they mastered the art of love manipulation or is it that they have capitalized on our brothers not being our sister's keepers? You always hear the women complaining about how South African men don't show them love, they don't spoil them, they don't respect them. That is why they have found love in foreign men. Yet when you look at a series of women that have gone for foreign men, not many can say they have really found love but instead found themselves in the lion's den per say. How do I explain this, I guess let me recite some of the stories I have seen and heard from close friends? Some of the stories have happened to me too. I will start with this story:

My friend Sandra had been very unlucky in love from the days back in university. I met her on my last year at university and we were staying together at the student residence. She was a bubbly young girl. What drew me to her was her warm heart and that contagious laugh that would just make everyone around her laugh. At the time I did not know her background story I was too pre-occupied with my studies and a relationship that was going through trials of its own. However, she was a great companion to hang with on the days I was not in class, work or with my boyfriend. I would cook and invite her to join me. She would always be this delight to be around, telling stories for days. Her stories would always attract so much attention that all other ladies from the other rooms in our res house even the ladies next

## Relationships with strings attached

door would come and join us, and we would have the time of our lives. She was also very hardworking, as a second-year student, she was already so focused that during school holidays she would work part-time at one of the major retail stores. This was something I had never done myself I only started working after graduating. All in all, she was a good person, committed, intelligent and hardworking any man would have been very lucky to have her as a wife.

Unfortunately, as we spent more and more time together, I realized she had been very unlucky when it came to love. She would meet a person who would be so interested in her only to leave her without an explanation. For the longest time I've known her she had not been able to keep a relationship for more than 3 months. Almost all the relationships ended the same, with the guys just going ghost on her, a term we did not know back then but someone termed it nicely in these current times. Everything would be great, great guy, good personality, communicating every day, they get together have the time of their life, be intimate then he just disappears or even ignores her like nothing ever happened. This was her story for some time, we would talk about that and pray this will look up one day. One day finally happened, she met this amazing guy who ticked all the boxes even came with an added bonus of being a supper romantic. He treated her like a queen from the beginning. I was so happy for her, by this time it had been 3 years since we knew each other. She was also now working permanently even had an apartment she was renting close to her work. I visited her once, the guy was there all sweet and romantic. I was really happy for her. Sometime went, because of our busy schedule we only communicated over the phone. Every time I would ask her about her amazing man, she would give me one quick answer, which was strange, but I paid no attention to it. They had been together for 2 years and I was very hopeful seeing he was her first long-term relationship.

One weekend she invited me to her apartment because she was about to move to a different one in a different area. When

## Relationships with strings attached

I arrived at her place, the guy was not there. I was like where is Mr. romantic. That is where she broke down and told me all the sob stories of how the guy was so supper romantic and loving in the beginning only to become an abusive manipulative monster. I could not believe she was talking about the same guy. As she sat there and recited all the crazy episodes of abuse she endured at the hands of this guy, I could not help but feel guilty for not being able to help my friend out of this situation. I was so hell bent on seeing her happy in a relationship that I could not even hear her silent cries in her one liner responses when I asked her about the guy.

Out of the many stories of abuse she endured from this guy there was one that stood out. The guy once beat her up throwing her all over the apartment, she was so hurt and bruised that she had to report at work that she was in a car accident. After beating her up like that the guy would still expect her to cook for his whole family that had moved into my friend's place, without her consent by the way. She said the guy would openly invite his family members (brothers, sisters, cousins, uncles, aunts etc.) to come stay with them when they come to South Africa for the first time. They would stay until they find their feet and get a place of their own.

While staying there my friend would be the one cooking in big pots serving the family like an unofficial "makoti". He would sometimes beat her up in front of the family members and they would not say anything. When the last family member had moved out, she finally plugged the courage to ask this man to leave her place. At this stage she could not carry on with the abusive relationship. He would go and come back after few weeks with gifts and empty promises of being a changed man. He even agreed to sign up for anger management classes as a sign of his new commitment to making things work with my friend. This went on for some time, he had now turned from a physical abuser to an emotional abuser. Because he would constantly do this disappearing and coming back and every time, he would come back he would come with gifts and sweet words.

## Relationships with strings attached

She would take him back only to endure hearing words of being called stupid, fat, ugly, and desperate to have a man in her life. He would even go as far as to say no man would ever want to be with her, he was just doing her a favour. In all of this he would still go with my friend to visit the family members that once lived in her flat. They were now living a lavish life, and he would be this sweet romantic guy as always. He would make promises that soon there will be having a huge wedding that will happen both here in South Africa and Cameroon in his hometown. My friend eventually got tired of the back and forth and the physical abuse that had resumed, she then applied for a protection order against this guy. He became so angry that he now started threatening her.

How she won this battle was by getting her brother to come and stay with her. After that the guy never had access to her place again. He could only try to get to her at work of which the security guards would not let him in. Eventually he disappeared. At this time my friend said she was happy and content with herself and all that she had been through, in fact life was moving along just fine. She got a promotion at work; bought a new car and was about to move to a better place, life was finally making sense. At this stage she was focused on her career, and she was doing great. I was happy that despite all the crazy she went through she was able to move past it, stay strong and still win in her career. We laughed at our growth and the lessons we learnt. By the time my visit was over I left her the happy soul that I had always known. I was happy she was over that crazy life and prayed she finds her match and in fact assured her there is someone out there that would be very happy and lucky to have her. Months went by, she moved and bought her first car as planned. Before I could see her and celebrate her new achievements she was moved to the Durban office by her company. At this time, she had started talking to a childhood friend whom she had dated briefly and broke up because of studying in different places. Years went by again without talking or linking up like friends should, but we always kept contact on important dates.

One day she called me excited that she was back in Pretoria she couldn't wait to come see me and the kids. We linked up and it was like we had never been apart. But the sad part was that yes, she had moved in her career, but relationship wise she was still stuck on zero, in fact the move back to Pretoria was a blessing in disguise for her because now she had lost everything. She had to start from scratch as in buying a bed to sleep on because of a relationship gone wrong. This time it was this childhood friend who came as a relationship only to use her till she was left with nothing. Remember she linked up with him months after she was finally over Mr. romantic abuser. They talked for months on the phone before they decided to date. The guy was working in Polokwane and would come visit her from time to time. Immediately when she moved to Durban, she managed to secure a well-paying job for this guy and he moved from Polokwane to Durban, to be with her as the job was in Durban. Things were fine at first until he started cheating and physically abusing her. I could not believe she had to go through that again. He would drive her car and cause accidents but not fix it, she always had to pick up the pieces. Throughout their time together he never contributed anything from his salary towards the house in fact everything in the house was accumulated by my friend ever since she started working. I could not understand how she lost everything until she told me when her company moved her back to Pretoria, she just left with a suitcase full of clothes. The aim was to come back for her things somehow although there was no plan. She had no choice but to move but she could not just say guy find a place I need to move with my things, so she just left like that.

For the first 3 months her company paid for accommodation as she was still looking for a place. She finally decided to purchase her first home, a stage in her life that was supposed to be celebrated however it was a sad reality, that when the 3 months ended, she would be faced with this huge house with no

## Relationships with strings attached

furniture. She was still in a relationship with this guy which was now long distance because of this move. This was not supposed to be a problem because they had done it before when he was working in Polokwane, in fact the guy was promising to ask for transfer to Pretoria hence they never really discussed the what will happen to her things. One day she drove to Durban for a visit. She drove all the way from Pretoria to Durban to only be told she can't get inside her own apartment. The reason she could not get inside was because the guy was now living with another woman, a woman that was apparently in this guy's life while they were together, they even have a child together. My friend says she had to drive back home the very same day. You just need to understand the distance from Pretoria to Durban is 617 km's, there are several tollgates in-between, and she had to do a return trip on the same day. She says she does not even know where she got the strength, but she did it without stopping anywhere and on this day, she made peace that she will never get her things back. I tried to convince her to cancel the lease, and I will ask a family friend to get her things, she was so weak, she said no friend I've made peace I bought a second-hand bed, fridge and couch it will do for now until I can buy new things again. She never got her things back but as years went, she managed to furnish her house slowly and eventually upgraded her car to an SUV. She was a strong woman after all. But before that a lot of crazy happened in her and my life.

Looking back, I ask myself were we too focused on finding that happy ending that we ended up attracting all these crazy men? Men that brought us nothing but misery and messed up our finances. We will hear my story later but for now I'm still telling her story. Well besides the sadness of what happened in Durban it was great to have my friend back and this time I was determined to be active in her life. We would have regular lunch, dinner and movie dates. She would come to my house and have pizza nights with the kids on her new healthy lifestyle cheat days. I forgot to mention that she had now decided to go on a healthy lifestyle journey, going to gym regularly, jogging every morning and evening and she was the go-to girl for healthy food recipes. Despite what she was facing she had lost a lot of weight looking good and glowing. Some days we would go to her house with the kids, and she would make us healthy meals and we would joke about the fact that she only has 1 plate, 1 glass, 1 spoon etc etc. She eventually had to buy extra plates and cutlery for the days we came to visit.

One time we would want to warm food and just stand there in the kitchen laughing because that is when she would remember that she left her microwave in Durban. My kids loved tea at that time, we would laugh again and say oh well let's boil water with the small pot because we know where the kettle is. She had to fight the battle of not wanting to buy a new microwave because she left a brand-new state of the art microwave in Durban. I would be the voice of reason reminding her that you refused for my people to forcefully get your things now make peace with those things let them go, life must move on we can't be warming food the old-fashioned way, buy that microwave, the next time I visit I am coming with microwave pop corns for the kids you don't want to disappoint them. That is how we eventually convinced her to slowly buy things for her house. For the most part we were happy until the urge to get a life partner comes along and we would retell each other our sob stories over and over again. One day I got the bright idea to match make her with another guy from Zambia that I met through another friend/business partner from DRC. I did this because she had been nagging me to match make because she was not having any luck the normal way. Well, I did not do proper vetting I just went with what I was told about the guy and my few interactions with him. He was a good guy struggled a bit with English, but he was decent and was in the trade business between his country and South Africa, so it meant he was this side very often.

This would give my friend time to get to know him and eliminate the clingy parasite nature of man she had attracted because he had to go back home for business. They met, hit it

## Relationships with strings attached

off and my friend (I don't know if it was thirst or what?) slept with the guy after the first date. After this happened it led to the guy confessing that he has a wife back home. That is where I failed her in the background testing, and I also hated him and the business partner for not telling me that. But I thanked him for telling my friend early before she was hooked as she ended whatever that was trying to start same time. The guy never stopped bringing her gifts like he did the first time they met, and he also did not even try to persuade my friend into a relationship with him they remained friends. I told my friend I am never match making for anyone ever again because I truly suck at it but I'm happy that this happened because as bad as it was it showed that she has now learned to put herself first. She had finally found love for herself. Well, that is what I thought anyways because what happened next in her life was the peak of her break down, I think.

Ok, months went we were in our happy routine in fact we were very happy. Looking back, we should not have wasted our time trying to figure out how such beautiful and successful women are still so single, we could have saved ourselves a lot of grief. It was December as always; I was back home visiting my mom with the kids. She calls me excited "my friend I just met a handsome guy while I was driving, it's crazy you won't believe this. I stopped at the robot (traffic lights) looked left there was this handsome guy staring at me. He followed me until I got to the gym then he parked next to me. At first, I thought its creepy what if this guy wants to steal my car or worse abduct me, so I came out and ran to the gym". I could not help but laugh at the running part because that was just typical of her, I just saw the drama in my head she was the drama queen after all. After I could contain my laugh, I told her to carry on, she was like "well guy followed me until I got to the gym door, and he said I'm sure you feel safe now may I please have your number. I gave it to him so quick and got inside the gym". We had a great laugh about the whole encounter, and I was so curious to hear where this was going. She said the guy called later that day explaining how he is new in town because he is opening a new up market club in the area in fact it was in the same complex as her gym. He sometimes sees her going to the gym. She now recalled that she recently started seeing construction happening in a place that was a restaurant near the complex entrance. He then asked to take her out sometime, of which she turned down as she was also going home for the December holidays to be with her father and sisters.

So, she said she had been texting with the guy every single day since they met. She has never chatted with any of her x's the way she talks to this guy. He is first to call in the morning and last to call at night and they would chat for hours. Most of the chats were business and work related which was a welcomed change because guy seemed very focused even advising her to start a business that he would support. Eventually December holidays ended, and we all had to go back to Pretoria. I could not wait to talk to her in person since she met this guy. She came back earlier than me and, in that time, she had been spending time with new guy who was from DRC by the way.

Their relationship seemed to have moved very fast because in the 2 weeks that they had met while I was home. They were now regulars at each other's places. After checking his lounges construction, he would come to her and sometimes sleep over and sometimes she would go sleep over at his place. When she was telling me about him, she was so happy saying guy is so loving and gentle even wants to cuddle the whole night after sex. She said for the first time ever she felt so happy and secure in his arms nothing else mattered in the world and the kisses and sex were just out of this world. I was so happy for her but in the back of my mind I was worried they were moving too fast, but he was way better than her past. He had his own place in an upmarket area, he was driving a range rover, so he was definitely not going to be a burden to her. Before the lounge opened my friend asked me to go with her to meet the guy as well as see his lounge. She also suggested we talk of possible business opportunities for my business. I went there and I was impressed at how the place looked, it was a place that I would also go to from time to time when I wanted to unwind. My friend was not a party or club scene person, but I could see how she was supporting him and how free she was in the lounge, we even sat and had few drinks during the day on a Tuesday which was definitely not us.

I finally met the guy; he was indeed handsome and charming we had a quick chat and they both took me around to see the place. We even went to the back to see the kitchen and he told me he is looking for someone to take over the kitchen if I'm interested. It looked like a great deal, but it was something I want to do in the future not when my finances are still a bit crazy. I wished both of them all the success, they had a great thing going. On this day apparently, guy asked my friend to take out a loan for him because he was waiting for money to buy stock and it was stuck somewhere, he assured her that once it was out, he would give her back that money and even pay for her other debts, he does not want his woman to be in debt. She told me this after she had already given the guy the money. My concerns came again, and I asked my friend all this time we have been struggling even boiling water with pots where did you get money to loan someone money for stock. She was like herself she does not know how it happened she found herself going to the bank applying for loan it got approved and she immediately transferred it to him. I knew how she does not like debts, and I could feel the anxiety in her voice that she had just did such a big thing for someone she just recently met. I tried to come her down and say let's pray he honours his word and pays her back. The anxiety quickly went away, and she invited me to the opening of the lounge. The big day came, and we went there had fun, but the guy was just distant he hardly even came to our table I just thought it's his big day probably busy making everyone happy. We had fun either way, had free drinks and went home after. It is at this stage now that my friend started experiencing Deja vu, the guy was no longer visiting her like usual she was no longer invited to his place.

## Relationships with strings attached

At this time everyone was probably back from December holidays. I started thinking probably this guy has a woman who probably went home for the holidays now she was back that's why he was so distant. But I quickly stopped those thoughts because wow that would be so bad for my friend not after she just gave him so much money. It happened for a few weeks now he was no longer picking up her calls some days, some days he would ask her to come meet him at the lounge and in that time, he would borrow her car to go get stock or go to his suppliers to pitch business. Now the only time they met was during the day when he needs her car for something. Or he would come for sex but never sleep over. Every time she asked him for her money, he would just dismiss it as his still waiting for the people and they are delaying giving him his money. One day she decided to go to the lounge unannounced during the day. When she got there the guy, and his manager were shocked to see her but downplayed it. They told her they are busy and took her to a table at the back and said they will bring her usual lunch. As she was sitting waiting a highly pregnant woman walked in caused havoc looking for her boyfriend, she was sitting at the back there shocked. The woman felt the need to come to her and tell her the sob story of how this guy got her pregnant and took her money now he is dodging her she was even carrying a gun prepared to shoot him but lost the courage as she does not want to go to jail pregnant like that.

My friend said she was just sitting there shocked. While sitting there she saw another old woman that was sitting at another table, and he keeps going to that table. When she looked closely, she realised that this woman was always at the lounge, and she talked to the staff like she was the one that hired them. Her investigative nature started kicking in, she went around enquiring only to find out that the woman was the main owner of the lounge, and the boyfriend was a co-owner or something like that. While waiting another woman came looking for him, that is when she decided to leave before even having her lunch. This was a start of a whole lot of crazy stories in this chapter of her life. Now we were back to square 1 with my friend confused at the current turn of events and it was not even the middle of February meaning it was only 2 months since she met this guy and already a lot had happened. I started advising her maybe she should cut ties with this guy because it seems he was nothing but trouble. Like classic abuser or classic narcissistic behaviour when she tried to cut ties that is when he love bombed her and gave her more empty promises even going as far as coming to sleep at her place when he closed the lounge late. The day I threw in the towel is when he took her car after she knocked off work and said he was going to get stock and bring back the car later in the evening. He never brought it back until the next day.

The next day she called me panicking because she had to go to work, and he was nowhere to be found. I asked her to track the car, and she managed to find it parked at the nearest bed and breakfast (BnB). went with her to assist her in picking up her car at that BnB. On our way there she decided that we go past his place first because I guess she did not want to believe it was him that spent the night at a BnB with her car. The security guards obviously refused for us to get in that Golf Estate, they also felt the need to tell us how stupid we were as South African women, by letting ourselves be played by foreign guys. They told us that this guy stays with that old woman who happens to also not be South African, the house belonged to her as well as the Range Rover. When she is not around the guy brings different women including my friend and he takes money and drives the cars of all these unsuspecting South African women. They also find out like us when it's too late and they have lost their money and dignity, that this foreign guy was playing them. They go on to mock us and say serves you right for thinking these foreign guys are better than us, that is when we decide ok, we've heard enough let us go to the BnB. When we get there, we find the car and we go to reception to ask them to look for him and ask him to give us the keys or we take the car because we have the spare keys. The lady at reception said it was against their policy to give us information of their guest and they unfortunately cannot also

## Relationships with strings attached

give us the car because it was registered in their guest's name. What we can do is to go to the police and open a case come back with the police that is the only time that they will be able to assist us.

We left. At this stage it was already 10 in the morning, and I realized we had both not applied for leave as we supposed to report before 9 according to both our company policy, so basically because of this guy our jobs were also at stake. We decided to trust God and not get any call from work, they would just think we are visiting clients. It took us almost an hour to finalise everything at the police station and the police agreed to accompany us because we know they love these domestic cases. When we arrived at the BnB the security guards were guarding the car because that's what we asked them, and guy was waiting for us and the police by the reception. He just came to my friend laughing and gave the police officer the car keys, he did not even want to talk to the police when they asked him why he took the car. He was now alone; after giving the car keys he went back to finish eating his breakfast alone. When we get to the car the security guards tell us he was there with 2 other cars, all cars were full of girls and guys. The guys and girls that came with him left with a bolt when we told them they can't drive the car the police are looking for it.

Our workday was over we were back at her place eating our sorrows away. I told this story to my business partner who was also Congolese, and he decided to let us create an event that will take money from this guy so that my friend can get her money back and cut her ties with this man for good. We had several meetings at my place with the team and the guy accepted the Congolese partner's event pitch. We were in full force of our event plan until we found out on the day of the event that my friend had met with the guy the day before and during their pillow talk gave him all the details of our plan.

Needless to say, our event went ahead but we did not make as much money as we planned. That's when I realized this guy's

## Relationships with strings attached

sex game was strong after all that drama my friend went back and even nearly cost me my company money. I decided to not partake in their relationship anymore until she finally saw the light on her own, when she met 2 other pregnant ladies who were also demanding their money from this guy, and they were coming from a different area meaning he had been going around Gauteng scamming women. One day my nanny told me her friend who got a job cleaning the lounge via my friend got beat up by her husband in full view of the community because he found her with the guy and other guys and girls at that BnB about to get in and do things that he can't even imagine. He had been following his wife for a week and realized that every day she says she is working late she goes there. He started telling everyone that my nanny gave her prostitution work. So, this guy was also sleeping with the waitresses and cleansers pimping them on top of the women he was scamming. That was when my friend made peace with him and the fact that her money was gone for good. At this point unfortunately, she did not want anything to do with men. One funny story she told me is that once a guy says hi to her, she just swears at him the same way you swear at a dog to leave you alone hahahahaha. Another friend met a guy from Malawi who came right at a time when she was having family issues. I don't know if this is spiritual or what, but the timing is always unreal. He came as a saviour in her life, promised her all that she wanted to hear. He even convinced her to move out of her mother's house because she was not good to her. Imagine the woman that gave birth to her and took care of her until old age was suddenly now a witch over her life. At the time of meeting this guy she had just given birth to a daughter whose father denied her when she was a few weeks pregnant. The new love promised to take care of both of them. For a few months he did but, in the process, made her get into financial obligations she would not have gotten into had she not moved out of her mom's house. In less than 4 months her new love even convinced her to quit her full-time government employment because she was destined for bigger things and her work was slowing her down. I am ashamed to say that I helped her write her resignation letter, but I did not have the full story. She only told me that she was resigning because she was not on good terms with her boss and things were getting worse. She didn't have any debts or obligations she had already secured a business, and her new man will help her out while she was waiting for her pension. I did try to convince her to wait for her business to be established before she resigns but she assured me that she had a good plan.

A month after she resigned the guy made up a story that he was going to do work outside the country where he would not be reachable because of the type of work he does. I found this very strange when I told my friend she was very much convinced that he was going to do work that is going to elevate them. I started being weary of this arrangement, but my friend was already unemployed waiting for her pension money. She was living with a small baby with no salary for food and rent. This was when she started borrowing money with the promise that she will pay back people as soon as her pension money came out. The guy would also occasionally pop up asking for money and she would give him. This went on until she was owing literally every loan shark in the town and her pension money delayed for some strange reason. She then decided to move to a different city closer to her company head office with hopes that it will fast-track her pension withdrawal. Even here she started new accounts of debts. At this stage she started losing her senses and there was no saving her even when you try to advise her to go back to work you would become her enemy and she would block you on her phone. Months went by and the guy was still not back from the secrete job. You would think my friend would wake up from the trans but instead she was deeper and deeper in love with this man. Her money eventually came out. The guy reappeared from the mystery assignment he was working on. He then convinced my friend to transfer all her pension into his account so as to start with the process of opening her business in a different city.

## Relationships with strings attached

She never got a chance to pay debts because the money never even stayed 2 days in her account. It's been 6 years now and my friend is still believing that this guy is coming back from wherever he went to. She is waiting for him to come and get her to live a life of luxury and great business deals that I don't even know if she even knew what kind of business she was investing in. This is really a summary of the years of misery she has been subjected to moving from house to house, living on the streets, in rural areas, etc. with her child by her side. At this stage, I found there are too many similar stories of South African ladies suffering at the hands of foreign love. If I could talk about the other stories my book would never end. At some point we wanted to do a series called foreign love because we might as well make money out of all these crazy stories that never seem to want to end because I can assure you if you can google such stories, you will find a fresh one.

Yes, my friends suffered from South African men too with the extreme being the Durban story, but the foreign stories were not any better. I found the issue is not really with the man but with the self-love, self-esteem and the illusion that many women suffer from that tells them that you are not complete until you have a man/husband by your side, and they go through great lengths to make this illusion a reality whilst forgetting what it is really costing them.

My wish is for woman to love themselves above the illusions and societal beliefs that are not founded upon what God says about them, it will save them from foreign and local love disappointments.

# ABOUT THE AUTHOR

Brenda Nomusa Molefe is a woman of many talents, but the creative industry has been always her biggest passion. Having successfully started and run a model agency that hosted fashion shows in the biggest business hub Province of Gauteng.

She is also a career Internal Auditor, a career she has loved since she fell in love with it when she was a student tutoring her fellow peers on the subject. She has reached a pinnacle in that career by being the first Chief Audit Executive for the Institute of Internal Auditors South Africa and the Leadership Academy for Guardians of Governance. She also has vast number of experiences in leadership roles in the Internal Auditing sphere of Provincial government both in Gauteng and KwaZulu Natal.

Her most important role though is being mother to her 3 beautiful kids. The love for writing and business saw her encouraging her daughter to writing her first fiction novel at the age of 13 and involving all her kids in the printing family business that she started in the year 2022.

Trials tried to break her, but she saw them as God preparing her for the greater purpose that He assigned in her and that is to spread the good news of the love that Jesus Christ has for all of us.

www.ingramcontent.com/pod-product-compliance
Lightning Source LLC
Chambersburg PA
CBHW062039290426
44109CB00026B/2667